Remarks on M. de Voltaire's History of Charles XII. King of Sweden. ... Interspersed With the Characters and History of Several Grand Visirs, and Other Officers of the Ottoman Empire. Written by Count Poniatowski, ... Translated Into English

REMARKS

ON

M. *de Voltaire's* Hiſtory

OF

CHARLES XII. King of *Sweden*.

In which not only a great Number of that Author's Miſtakes are rectified, but many of his Omiſſions are largely ſupplied, Series of Tranſactions are otherwiſe related than in him, or any other Writer; and ſeveral curious Particulars, no where elſe to be found, concerning the Battle of *Pultawa*, the King's Flight into *Turkey*, the Action and Peace at the River *Pruth*, the Intrigues and Negociations at the *Porte*, &c. are recorded.

Interſperſed with the Characters and Hiſtory of ſeveral Grand Viſirs, and other Officers of the *Ottoman* Empire.

Written by Count PONIATOWSKI, a *Poliſh* Nobleman, formerly Lieutenant-General to his *Swediſh* Majeſty, and his Miniſter at the *Porte* during that King's Reſidence in *Turkey*, now Lieutenant-General in the Service of *Poland*.

Tranſlated into E N G L I S H.

L O N D O N:

Printed for J. BRINDLEY, Bookſeller to his Royal Highneſs the Prince of WALES, at the *King's-Arms* in *New-Bond-Street*, and J. HODGES, at the *Looking Glaſs* over againſt St *Magnus's* Church, *London-Bridge*, and ſold by T. COOPER, at the *Globe* in *Pater-noſter-Row*. Price 2 s.

M DCC XLI.

THE
EDITOR'S PREFACE.

O N E *of our ancient Wits said very
agreeably, but in a Manner perhaps
a little too decisive, that,* a Man
must be very weak, who studied
History with the Hope of disco-
vering in it what had passed ; be-
cause, it is not so much the History of Facts, as
of the Opinions which such and such Authors
have conceived of them, and of the *Relations
which they have published* (a) *We are almost tempt-
ed to believe him, when we see not only the Negligence
and Inattention, but even the Infidelity, and want of
Exactness, with which it is most frequently writ.*

*In Fact, among the prodigious Number of Wri-
ters of all Kinds, who have attempted it, there are
absolutely but a very few who are truly worthy of
the Attention and Approbation of Men of Sense.
This is what Criticks the least severe, and the most
judicious, have but too solidly proved.*

To turn to the Ancients, we reckon but a very few
Thucydides *and* Polybius's, *among the* Greeks ;
and but a very few Sallusts, Suetonius's *and* Tacitus's
among the Romans. *And of the Moderns, for one*
Thuanus, *and 'one* Grotius, *who were two in-
comparable Men, we have Millions of* Varillas's
and Maimbourgs *They are sometimes, indeed,
agreeable Writers ; but, for the most Part, destitute of the most essential Qualities, Sincerity and
Learning, and consequently very bad Historians :* Men
who are ready, not only to publish with Precipita-

(a) **Oeuvres de l'Abbé de St. Real,** tom. III p 171.

PREFACE.

tion the History of the first Hero that is proposed to them, even while he yet lies publickly expofed upon his Bed of State, *as has been judicionfly obferved* (b) ; *but alfo to lye moft impudently in his Favour, either from Intereft or Spirit of Party, and very often from both.*

It is not without Reafon, therefore, that Readers of Underftanding turn over with Abundance of Circumfpection the many hiftorical Writings that are daily publifhed, even thofe towards which one would imagine they muft be the moft favourably difpofed; becaufe this Precaution, and this Diffidence, are unhappily but too well founded.

When Mr. de Voltaire *publifhed his Hiftory of* Charles XII, *King of* Sweden ; *the Talents of the Author; the Impartiality, hwas reafonably fuppofed to have, with regard to Princes and People from whom he had nothing to hope or fear; the Public Proteftations that he made of his Love of Truth, at the Head of his Work, the illuftriousPerfons he there cites as his Guarantees, and from whom he affures us he obtained his Memoirs* (c) ; *every Thing, in a Word, contributed to form the moft advantageous Prejudice in his Favour His Hiftory, accordingly, was extremely well received, and almoft univerallyapplauded.But yet, Thing every in it was very far from being as true, and as exact, as could have been wifhed. Not to mention the Obfervations of Meffieurs* de la Mottaye *and* d'Aldeifield, *you*

(b) *Journal hiftor. de la Repub, des Lettres,* tom III p 152
(c) Thefe Perfons were, M *Fabricius,* who lived feven Years in clofe Familiarity with King *Charles XII* and retired into *England* a long Time after his Death , M *Croiffy,* the *French* Embaffador to that Monarch , M *de Fierville,* the *French* Envoy to him in *Turkey*, M. *deFeriol,* Embaffador to the *Ottoman Porte* , M *de Ville Longue,* a Colonel in his Service , M. *de Poniatowski* , and, in fhort, fometimes crowned Heads themfelves See the preliminary Difcourfe to his Hiftory, in the *French.*

have

PREFACE.

have here the Remarks of a Polish *Nobleman*, and perhaps of one of those illustrious *Guarantees*, with whose Names *Mr*. de Voltaire does himself Honour ; in which many *Facts* are related quite differently from what we find them in him, and in some *Particulars*, where that *Author* brings himself as a sort of ocular *Witness* of what he relates.

For Example, *M*. de Voltaire *says*, p. 172. That *Poniatowski* entered into close Friendship with one *Bru*, a *Frenchman*, who had been Chancellor of the *French* Embassy. *But our* Polish *Lord remarks here*, p 40. *That* this Friendship was with an old *Hungarian* Gentleman, named *Ferens Hornat*, and a Refugee at *Constantinople*. *In the same Page*, *M*. de Voltaire *expresses himself thus*. One who seconded *Poniatowski's* Designs with the greatest Abilities, was *Fonseca*, a *Portuguese* Physician and *Jew*, whom I knew very well at *Paris*, but who was then settled at *Constantinople*. *But the* Polish *Lord attributes this to a French* Renegade, the chief Surgeon of the Seraglio, whose Name was *Goin*

This surprising Diversity is not only remarked with respect to Persons, as well in their own Names as in the Names of their Countries, but even in long and circumstantial Recitals of Facts Witness, among others, that of the Motive which induced Charles XII to renounce Wine for ever, which our noble Pole, in p. 3, and 4. in plain Terms ascribes to the Indecencies that Liquor had made him commit ; but which M de Voltaire, p. 26, contents himself to say, was owing merely to its over heating Constitution, which was already all on fire. And witness also the King of Sweden's pretended Letter to the Grand Signior, recited by M. de Voltaire, p 169, 170 ; but which our Nobleman, p. 39 affirms to have been quite otherwise, and that Charles XII, the sworn Enemy of all Flattery,

A 2   never

PREFACE.

never signed a Letter so full of Vanity and Osten‐
tation.'

It is the same with regard to many brilliant
Touches, *and* extraordinary Particulars, *where‐
with Mr.* de Voltaire *has thought proper to en‐
rich and adorn his Book ; of which not a Word is
said here, or the little Reality of which is here
shewn. And the same Thing may be also said of
many considerable Omissions, that have been the
more carefully supplied in the present Work, in pro‐
portion as they are essential to this History.*

*We shall not detain the Reader with any needless
Encomiums on these Remarks. As they are natu‐
rally writ, without any studied Affectation of Stile,
and with that native Candor, which makes a fa‐
vourable Impression upon every equitable Reader,
they cannot fail of being agreeably received by the
Publick , especially as they come from a Man of
Rank and Distinction, who writes as a* Cotem‐
porary *that is well informed,* not by *other* Co‐
temporaries, *but by his own Eyes , and who might,
perhaps much more justly than Mr.* de Voltaire,
boast of having his Information sometimes from
crowned Heads. ———— Thus far the Editor.

The Translator has only to add, that whereas
in the Orignal References are made to two
Editions of Mr. *de Voltaire's* History that of *Basil*
in 1731, and that of *Amsterdam* in 1739, it was
thought sufficient here to refer to the *Amsterdam*
Edition only, as the most common in *England*,
and to the *English* Translation If any one
should wonder at seeing Mr. *de Voltaire's* Ori‐
ginal taken Notice of here at all, let him compare
the Passages commented on with the Pages re‐
ferred to in the *English* Translation, and he will see
that there was no other Way of justifying some Va‐
riations from the latter, but by sending him where
he may be sure of finding his Author perfect and
exact. R E‐

REMARKS

ON

M. *de Voltaire*'s Hiſtory

OF

CHARLES XII. King of *Sweden.*

M. *de Voltaire*'s Text.

Page 22 of the *Amſterdam* Edition of the Original, 1739. p. 15. of the *Engliſh* Tranſlation in 12mo. the 6th Edition, 1735.

HREE *powerful Princes, taking the Advantage of his* (King Charles's) *extreme Youth, conſpired his Ruin almoſt at the ſame Time. The firſt was* Frederick IV. *King of* Denmark, *his Couſin. The ſecond,* Auguſtus, *Elector of* Saxony, *and King of* Poland: Peter the Great, *Czar of* Muſcovy, *was the third, and the moſt dangerous.*

REMARK.

THE Valour of the *Swediſh* Nation has been acknowledged in all Ages. Their Kings have ever been great Warriors, and their Reputation has been juſtly eſtabliſhed for a long Time paſt.

B

But,

But, the extreme Youth of *Charles* XII, his Occupations at the Beginning of his Reign, his Propenfity to Pleafures and Diverfions, a profound Peace which the *Swedes* had enjoyed for a great Number of Years, made the Czar, and the Kings of *Poland* and *Denmark,* imagine to themfelves the Facility of depreffing that Power, and making Conquefts upon it.

However, as fome Pretences were neceffary to begin a War, the Czar took up that of not having been honourably received in his Paffage through *Riga,* though he was there *incognito* · The King of *Poland* found that of the *Pacta conventa,* by which he was obliged to take and rejoin to *Poland,* all the Provinces and Countries which that Kingdom had loft ; and *Livonia* was one of thofe Provinces : The King of *Denmark* thought to ftrip the Duke of *Holftein-Gottorp* of his Eftates , not doubting but the King of *Sweden* would be overwhelmed himfelf, if he attempted to fuccour the Duke, his Relation and Ally.

Thefe Princes made a very private League among themfelves, and took their Meafures for beginning the War; judging, that a young Prince without Experience, with Troops enervated by a long Peace, would be unable to refift their Efforts. This was the true Subject of the Northern War.

M. *de Voltaire's* Text.
Amfterdam Edition, p 52. *Englifh* Tranflation,
p. 25.

He determined alfo to abftain from Wine all the reft of his Life , not, as has been pretended, to punifh himfelf for an Excefs, which, as they fay, led him into fome Irregularities, unworthy of himfelf. Nothing is more falfe than this vulgar Report. He never fuffered Wine to get the Maftery
over

over his Reason; as I have been assured by M. de Croissy, Ambassador (of France) at his Court. But Wine over-heated his Constitution, which was already all Fire. He soon after left off Beer too, and confined himself to pure Water.

REMARK.

CHARLES the Twelfth's Abstinence from Wine, according to the Report of many Persons, who were, from the earliest Youth of that Prince, very near his Person, was occasioned by the Reproaches of the Queen his Grandmother. One Day, when the King came home from Hunting, and had drank Wine a little copiously at Breakfast, he went to wait upon the Queen at her Dinner, quite tipsy, and besmeared with the Blood of the Beasts they had killed. The Queen reproved him very severely for his Indecency; but, not caring to listen to a Correction so rough, and his Spur being, either with Design, or thro' Negligence, hung in the Table-Cloth, he went out of the Room hastily, and threw down all the Dishes upon her Majesty's Clothes. At Dinner-Time the next Day, the Queen began to renew her Reprimands, reproaching him with his Excess of Wine. *Charles* rose up, went to the Buffet, ordered a large Glass of Wine to be filled him, and drank it off to the Queen's Health; saying at the same Time, That, ' since Wine ' had made him deficient in the Respect he ' owed her, it was for the last Time in his Life ' that he now drank of it.' And, in effect, he kept his Word.

M. *de Voltaire's* Text.
Amsterdam Edition, p. 54. *English* Translation, p. 26.
While the little Country of Holstein *was thus the*

Seat

Seat of the War, two Squadrons, one from Eng-land, *and the other from* Holland, *appeared in the* Baltick-Sea. *These two States were Guarantees of the Treaty of* Altena, *which the Danes had violated. The Interest of their Commerce has a long Time engaged the* English *and* Dutch, *as far as lies in their Power, to preserve an equal Ballance among the Princes of the North. They joined the young King of* Sweden, *who seemed in Danger of being over-whelmed by so many united Enemies, and succoured him for the same Reason that the others attacked him, because they thought him not in a Condition to defend himself.*

REMARK.

IN Acknowledgment for the Support of the King of *England*, *Charles* XII promised that Nation, that he would not intermeddle in the War with *France* for a certain Number of Years. The Remembrance of this Promise very much favoured the Negociation of the Duke of *Marlborough* in *Saxony.*

M. *de Voltaire's* Text.
Amsterdam Edition, p 84. *English* Translation, p. 47.
  Charles *very soon got his Cannon landed, and formed his Army, while the Enemy, blinded by the Smoke, were not able to oppose him, except by a few Shot discharged at Random.*

REMARK.

CHARLES XII could land only two Regiments of Infantry, the Body of *Drabans*, consisting of 200 Men, and a Squadron of Cuirassiers of his own Regiment. It was with this Handful of Men that he beat the Enemy.

M. de

Mr. *de Voltaire*'s Text.
Amsterdam Edition, p 116, *English* Translation,
p. 67

The King of Sweden *at last arrived before War-*
saw, on the 5th of May 1702. *The Gates were*
opened to him upon the first Summons. He sent a-
way the Polish Garrison, dismissed the City-Guard,
and every where established Guards of his own ——
King Augustus *was then getting togethre his Forces*
at Cracow. *He was much surprised to see the*
Cardinal Primate arrive there?

R E M A R K.

WARSAW was not fortified, nor was
there any Garrison there. The Cardinal
continued in the Place of his Residence at *Louiez*,
and did not go to *Cracow*.

M *de Voltaire*'s Text.
Amsterdam Edition, p. 119, 120. *English* Translation, p. 69, 70.

Charles *gained a compleat Victory.* —— *He made*
no Stay upon the Field of Battle, but march'd di-
rectly to Cracow. —— *He departed from that City*
in the Resolution of pursuing Augustus *without*
Intermission. But some Miles from the City his
Horse fell with him, and broke his Thigh They
were obliged to carry him back to Cracow, *where*
he remained for six Weeks in the Hands of his
Surgeons.

R E M A R K.

HE staid eight Days on the Field of Battle;
then left all the Wounded in the Castle of
Pinczow, at the Distance of a League from the
said Field: Afterwards he marched to *Cracow*,
where

where he broke his Leg, and continued there the Time mentioned, for a Cure.

Mr. *de Voltaire*'s Text.
Amſterdam Edition, p. 123. *Engliſh* Tranſlation, p. 72.

Ch*a*les, *having augmented his Troops with ſix Thouſand Horſe,* — *march'd againſt the* Saxon *Army,* — *which ſhunned his Approach, and retired towards* Pruſſia.

REMARK.

THE ſix Thouſand Men of whom the Author ſpeaks, brought from *Pomerania* by General Count *Guldenſterna,* were ſent back from whence they came. In their March, a Party of *Poles,* commanded by Colonel *Rzevowſki,* fell upon a Detachment of two Hundred Horſe, and made them Priſoners. Upon this News the King of *Sweden,* who had ſtopped at *Lubnice* in the Palatinate of *Sendomir,* to get more perfectly recovered of his Fall, diſpatched Count *Pomatowſki* to General *Lubomirſki,* with Orders to tell him, ' That if ' he did not ſend back the two Hundred Men ' that had been carried off, he would cauſe all his ' Eſtates to be ravaged, and laid in Aſhes.' This had its Effect, and the Priſoners were all delivered.

Mr. *de Voltaire*'s Text.
Amſterdam Edition, p. 120, 121. *Engliſh* Tranſlation, p 70.

In this ſhort Interval, Auguſtus *aſſembles firſt at* Mariembourg, *then at* Lublin, *all the Orders of the Kingdom, who had been before convoked at* Sendomir. — *He there regained almoſt all their Minds by Preſents and Promiſes, and by that Affability, which is ſo neceſſary to abſolute Kings to win their*

their Subjects Affections, and to elective Kings to preserve their Authority.

REMARK.

HERE a Circumstance, very neceſſary for the clearing up of the Hiſtory, is omitted. The Deputies of *Great Poland*, upon a Suſpicion of their being in the Intereſt of the King of *Sweden*, were not admitted to give their Votes in the Diet of *Lublin*. In the Dietine of Report, an Aſſembly uſually held after the Diet, they exaggerated the Affront given to the *Palatinates*; and the Invaſion made on their Liberty. Animated, moreover, and ſupported by the *Swedes*, they entered into a Confederacy, by which they engaged to maintain King *Auguſtus* upon the Throne, *Salvis juribus pactorum conventorum*; a Clauſe that was very liable to Criticiſm, and a doubtful Interpretation, if the King had taken notice of it. This Confederacy, calling in other *Palatinates* to join that of *Great Poland*, advanced towards *Warſaw*, where, in the Aſſembly convoked by the Cardinal, the *Exvinculation* of their Obedience to the King of *Poland* was publiſhed.

Mr. *de Voltaire*'s Text.
Amſterdam Edition, p. 120, & *ſeq*. *Engliſh* Tranſlation, p. 84, & *ſeq*.
When the Primate of Poland *knew that* Charles XII *had nominated the* Palatine Leczinski, *in the ſame arbitrary Manner that* Alexander *nominated* Abdolominus, *he immediately waited on his Majeſty, to endeavour to make him change his Reſolution, and transfer the Crown to one* Lubomirski. ' *But what, ſays the Conqueror, have you to object againſt* Staniſlaus Leczinſki ?' ' *Sir, ſays the Primate, he is too young*'. *The King replied,* ' *He is much about my Age,*

*Age,' turned his back upon the Prelate, and imme-
diately sent Count* Hoorn *to signify to the Assembly at*
Warsaw, *that they must elect a King in five Days,
and that the Election must fall on* Staniflaus Leczin-
fki. *Count* Hoorn *arrived the 7th of* July, *and fixed the Day of Election to the 12th, as if he had
ordered the Decampment of a Battalion. —— The
Bishop of* Polnania *put an End to the Assembly by
declaring, in the Name of the Diet,* Staniflaus *e-
lected King of* Poland *Charles, who had mixed
with the Crowd, was the first to cry out* Vivat. *All
the Hats flew up into the Air, and the Noise of the
Acclamations quite stifled the Cries of the Op-
posers.*

R E M A R K.

IT was Count *Hoorn,* Ambassador of *Sweden*
to the Assembly at *Warsaw,* who demanded
of the Cardinal the Election of a Candidate to
the Throne of *Poland* The Cardinal's Propofitions, and the Answer he received to them, were
conformable to the Author's Relation.

For a long Time before this, the Cardinal had
wished to see his Cousin *Towianski* (now great
Chamberlain of the Crown, and actually refiding
privately at *Paris*) married to the Daughter of the
Great General of the Crown *Lubomirski.* The Pro-
posal had been hitherto rejected, but was now, in
the present Situation of Affairs, accepted of,
through the Interposition of the Palatine of
Polnania.

The Cardinal, vexed that the King had expressed himself so positively with regard to the
Choice of a Candidate, endeavoured, but in vain,
to make him change his Sentiments in favour of
the Father-in-Law of his Relation

The Time of Convocation expired, and the
King pressed on the Election upon the Day fixed by the Cardinal's *Universalia.* The

The King of *Sweden* was not prefent, as the Author fays, in the Field of Election ; nor was any one of his Deputies there : He ftaid in his Camp three Leagues from *Warfaw.*

M. *de Voltaire*'s Text.
Amfterdam Edition, p. 150. *Englifh* Tranflation, p. 90.

Charles, *accompanied by King* Staniflaus, *went in queft of his Enemy* (Auguftus) *at the Head of the beft Part of his Troops. The* Saxon *Army fled every where before him.— Succeffes became too familiar to him. He faid it was rather Hunting than Fighting, and complained that he could not purchafe a Victory.*

REMARK.

THE King of *Sweden*, at his Return from *Leopol*, found King *Auguftus* at *Warfaw. Charles* encamped at *Prag*, on the other Side of the *Viftula* ; and thefe two Princes, feparated by the River, often took a View of each other, and once even fpoke together, each being on his own Side of the River.

The Preparations which the King of *Sweden* made for building a Bridge, occafioned the King of *Poland* to quit *Warfaw,* to keep out of his Way.

M. *de Voltaire*'s Text.
Amfterdam Edition, p. 151. *Englifh* Tranflation, p. 91.

Count Schullenbourg, *a very able General — made War with Addrefs, and the two Kings with Vivacity. — After many Stratagems and Counter-marches, — the* Swedes *fell upon the* Saxons *with their ufual Impetuofity, who waited for them unfhaken. —* Schullenbourg *gave way at laft ; but his Troops*

C were

were not broken, — and the Saxons *croſſed the* Oder *upon Planks, under Favour of the Night.*

REMARK.

THE King of *Sweden* made incredible Expedition, with ſeven Regiments of Dragoons, to follow the *Saxons* · It was then that he attacked General *Schullenbourg* at the Diſtance of a League from the Frontiers of *Sileſia.* The *Swedes* entered into the Enemies Square ; but they did not avail them of that Advantage, becauſe of the Obſcurity of the Night, which permitted General *Schullenbourg* to make an honourable Retreat, and ſave his Troops.

The King of *Sweden,* at Break of Day; went in purſuit of his Enemies ; but, perceiving that they had already paſſed the River, he turned back to re-enter *Poland,* and put himſelf firſt into Winter Quarters.

Two Hundred unfortunate *Coſſacks,* of General *Schullenbourg*'s Army, being ſurpriſed in a Village by the *Swedes,* attempted to defend themſelves in the Houſes, but the Houſes in the mean Time taking Fire, ſome of them were burned, and the reſt put to the Sword.

M. *de Voltaire*'s Text.
Amſterdam Edition, p. 157, *& ſeq.* *Engliſh* Tranſlation, p 97, *& ſeq.*

Stanſlaus *prepared for his Coronation, which was quietly and pompouſly performed* October *the 4th,* 1705, *in the City of* Warſaw, *notwithſtanding it had been the Cuſtom in* Poland *to crown their Kings at* Cracow. — Cha les XII *was preſent at this Ceremony Incognito, as he had been at the Election ; the only Fruit he reaped from his Conqueſts.*

R E-

REMARK.

WHEN the Day of King *Staniſlaus*'s Co-ronation drew near, the King of *Sweden* ſent before him two Regiments of Horſe, com-manded by the Colonels *Nirod* and *Burnſchild*, to take Poſt at *Warſaw*.

Five Thouſand *Saxons*, under the Command of General *Patkul*, and a Party of *Poliſh* Troops, making together near 12,000 Men, paſſed the *Viſtula*, and attacked the *Swedes*. Theſe not only defended themſelves, but defeated the Enemy, took General *Patkul*, and forced the *Poles* to repaſs the *Viſtula* by ſwimming.

King *Staniſlaus* arrived at *Warſaw* ſome Days after this Action, as did alſo the King of *Sweden*; and the Coronation ſoon followed

Before he ſet out from *Ravitz* for *Warſaw*, the King of *Sweden* ordered Count *Poniatowſki* to ſelect two hundred *Swedes*, to form a Body-Guard for King *Staniſlaus*, under Command of that Count.

While the Ceremony of the Coronation was performing at *Warſaw*, the Czar aſſembled his Troops at *Grodno*, in Conjunction with King *Auguſtus*. The King of *Sweden*, being informed of this, marched with King *Staniſlaus*, in the Depth of Winter, to attack them.

The *Muſcovites* had fortified themſelves at *Grodno*, and entrenched up to the Teeth. Forty thouſand Infantry, ſupported by the Preſence of two Monarchs, were there ſhut up. But the Czar and King *Auguſtus* retired, at the unexpected Ap-proach of the King of *Sweden*, and left all their Infantry to themſelves.

The King of *Sweden* came before the Place two Days after; but the ſevere Froſts, and ſuch a nu-merous Garriſon, on the one Hand, and a preci-pitate March, which had extremely fatigued the *Swediſh* Troops, added to the Want of Provi-

ſions,

fions, on the other, obliged *Charles* XII to put
into Quarters, and difperfe his Troops for twelve
Leagues round, in expectation of a more proper
Seafon for the Attack.

No fooner did it begin to thaw, but the *Mufcovites* decamped from *Grodno*, and took their
Route, by long Marches, through *Polefia* towards
Volhinia; a Way that was croffed by many Ri-
vers, and full of almoft impaffable Moraffes.

The King of *Sweden*, having received Information of it, purfued them, not without incredible
Pains, in a Seafon fo difagreeable that his Men
marched up to their Knees in Mud. He pierced
quite into *Volhinia*; but, feeing his March was
fruitlefs, and that, in a Country fo vaft, his Purfuit would have been endlefs, he made a Halt
there to repofe his Troops, which were extremely
fatigued. He came up at laft with the Rear-
Guard of the Enemy, and defeated it, but the
Grofs of their Army efcaped. It was here he took
the Refolution, in order to put an end to the
War, to march directly into *Saxony*.

This Project was executed, after a faint Oppo-
fition from the *Saxons*, in which they were defeated. It was this that obliged King *Auguftus* to fend
two of his Minifters, *Imhoff* and *Fingftein*, to the
Conqueror, to fue for Peace, which was granted
him on very heavy Conditions, that are known
to all the World. General *Schullenbourg* had been
juft before defeated by Count *Reinfchild*, who ftaid
behind in *Great Poland* with a Body of 8,000
Men.

M. *de Voltaire*'s Text.

Amfterdam Edition, p. 199. *Englifh* Tranflation, **123**.

Charles *had given his Word in* 1700, *not to intermeddle in the War of* Lewis XIV *with the Allies.*
But

But the Duke of Marlborough *did not believe there was a Prince so much a Slave to his Word, as not to sacrifice it to his Grandeur and Interest.*

REMARK.

CHARLES XII, having learned the Uneasiness of the Duke of *Marlborough*, on his being unable to discover whether that King's Intentions were to unite with *France* ; his Majesty ordered Baron *Gortz* to tell the Duke, that he remembered his Word given in 1700, and that the Time was not yet come for him to meddle with their War.

M. *de Voltaire*'s Text
Amsterdam Edition, p. 215, 216. *English* Translation, p. 133.

The King of Sweden, *in the midst of his victorious March, received a solemn Embassy from the* Turks.—*The Ambassador presented* Charles *with an hundred* Swedish *Soldiers, who, having been taken by the* Calmucks, *and sold into* Turkey, *were redeemed by the Grand Seignior, and now sent by that Emperor to the King, as the most agreeable Present he could make him.*

REMARK.

HERE the Author is mistaken: For it was not the *Turkish* Ambassador, who presented the King with Slaves made by the *Muscovites*; but it was the King of *Sweden*, who, when he had taken *Leopol*, found there an hundred *Turkish* Slaves, taken formerly in their Wars with the *Poles*, and gave them their Liberty, a Sum of Money, magnificent Habits, and an Escorte to the Frontiers of *Turkey*.

The

The *Turkish* Ambaſſador offered the King an Alliance with his Maſter. But, whether that Prince thought himſelf ſufficiently ſtrong alone to finiſh his War with the Czar, or whether he was perſuaded, by the Repreſentations of the Clergy about him, that it was not proper to make an Alliance with the Enemies of Chriſtianity, he contented himſelf with ſending back the Ambaſſador loaded with Preſents, without giving him a Word of Anſwer to his Propoſitions.

Mr. *de Voltaire*'s Text.

Amſterdam Edition, p. 233, 234. *Engliſh* Tranſlation, p. 144.

They found a Body of Muſcovites *advancing towards the other Side of the River The King was aſtoniſhed, but reſolved immediately to paſs the* Deſna, *and attack the Enemy The Banks of this River were ſo ſteep, that they were obliged to let down the Soldiers with Cords. —— The Body of* Muſcovites, *which arrived at the ſame Time, were not above eight thouſand Men; ſo that they made but ſmall Reſiſtance, and this Obſtacle was alſo ſurmounted.*

REMARK.

TWenty thouſand *Ruſſians* were entrenched on the Banks of the ſaid River, which were very marſhy. The King paſſing over on Foot, at the Head of his Regiment of Guards, attacked them, forced their Entrenchment, and drove the Enemies quite into a thick Wood, which lay behind them.

As the *Swedes*, in paſſing the River, could preſerve no more than that one Charge which was in their loaded Fuſils, the Reſt of their Ammunition being ſo wetted, that they could not uſe the Powder; it was with Sword in Hand, and at the Pike's End, that they fought. In this Action, the

the greateſt Part of the Officers being killed or wounded, the King ſeeing Count *Guldenſterna* fall, the only Officer that commanded a Battalion, put himſelf at the Head of it, Sword in Hand, and charged the Enemies Battalions

Upon this the Soldiers cried out aloud, begging the King to retire; aſſuring him, that they would perform their Duty by themſelves: But that Prince would not liſten to them, and finiſhed the Victory by his own Valour and Intrepidity.

Prince *Menzikoff* was come up with ten thouſand Dragoons, to ſupport the Infantry. An hundred and fifty of the King of *Sweden*'s Drabans, a Squadron of an hundred and twenty five Horſe of the Regiment of Cuiraſſiers, and a Squadron of the Body Dragoons, which had found a Paſſage at ſome Diſtance, attacked Prince *Menzikoff*, ranged as he was in Order of Battle, ſo briskly, that they broke his Ranks, and drove him into the Wood.

In this Action fell General *Wrangel*, Commander of the Drabans, ſixty five of his Men, a hundred Dragoons, and as many of the little Troop of *Swediſh* Horſe; having the Glory, in Death, to have beaten and drove before them ſo many thouſand Enemies.

But ſuch Actions as theſe were nothing new among the *Swedes*. Count *Reinſchild*, for Example, being then in the Palatinate of *Sendomir*, detached Major *Wolffrath* with three hundred Cavalry to the Diſtance of a League and a half from the Army. Some thouſands of the *Saxon* and *Poliſh* Troops, who had agreed to try their Fortune on *Reinſchild* himſelf, fell in with Major *Wolffrath*, and quite ſurrounded him. This *Swediſh* Officer, ſeeing no Poſſibility of his being ſuccoured, reſolved bravely to make his way out of the Encloſure, clofuie, in which he was hemmed up. Having divided his Men into fmall Troops, that he might extend them the moie, he fell defperately upon the Enemy's Body, had the good Fortune to make his way thro' it, and retired to the Camp with a hundred and twenty Men, the reft having been killed, and of thefe hundred and twenty who came off, there was not one without a Wound, the Major having the fame Fate as the reft.

An Action fo bold made the Enemy coolly reflect, and retire without attempting any Thing againft *Reinfchild*. We muft do this Juftice to the Valour of the *Swedifh* Nation, to own, that an Officer needed no more than to look behind him ; provided he paid them with his Prefence, he was fuie of being followed by his Tioops in the greateft Dangers

The King of *Sweden*, with fo many fine Qualities, had another yet that was very laudable. He never made an Officer accountable for the Event of an Action , provided he had done his Duty, whether he had beat or was beaten, he was iewarded. Witnefs Lieutenant-Colonel *Kreyts*, who being commanded, with eight hundied Horfe, to fome Leagues Diftance from *Thorn*, was furprized and defeated by the Enemies, after he had fought well and made a good Defence. At his Return from this Action he was made a Colonel. No Officei was ever advanced, but according to his Merit.

Mr. *de Voltaire*'s Text.

Amfterdam Edition, p. 235, & *feq. Englifh* Tranflation, p. 145.

General Levenhaupt *had already paffed the* Borifthenes *above* Mohilow, *and was advancet twenty Leagues into the* Ukrania. — *The Czar ap* peared at the Head of fifty thoufand Men.

R E

REMARK.

THE *Boriſthenes* about *Mohilow*, does not make the Frontier of *Poland*; the Palatinate of *Miciſlaw* extends farther, to within ſome Leagues of *Smolensko*

The Czar, having paſſed the *Boriſthenes*, ſet every Thing on Fire, and burned above thirty Leagues of the Country, as well of that belonging to *Poland* as of his own, to deprive the *Swedes* of all Subſiſtence, and hinder the Purſuit.

After ſome Days March, not one of which paſſed without ſome Action with the Enemies, which had no other Effect than to leſſen the Number of the *Swedes*, though the Advantage was always on their Side, the King being abſolutely deſtitute of Provifions, was obliged to ſlacken a Purſuit that would have entirely ruined him, and took the Reſolution to turn back, in order to throw himſelf into *Muſcovite Ukrania*, a fertile and plentiful Country , eſpecially as he had a good Underſtanding with *Mazeppa*, General of the *Coſſacks*, who promiſed, by a private Correſpondence which he kept up with the King, to ſubmit to him, with all his Country, and favour his Expedition.

As the *Ukrania* is ſeparated from *Poland* by the River *Soſſa*, and a very thick Foreſt about thirty Leagues in length, interſected with a Number of Moraſſes, the King ordered out a Detachment of five Thouſand Men, under the Command of Major-General *Leger-Crona*, his Aid-de-Camp General, with the Flower of the Subaltern Officers, to advance before the Army, make a Bridge upon that River, open the Paſſage of the Foreſt, and haſten to take Poſſeſſion of a Poſt called *Poczop*, the only Way by which his Enemies could penetrate into *Ukrania*. But this General,

D   by

by a Fatality of one Side, and by his own Fault and Negligence on the other, not having taken fufficient Care to furnifh himfelf with good Guides; this General, I fay, after having paffed the River, inftead of marching towards *Poczop*, took, at the Entrance of the Foreft, a quite contrary Way, above thirty Leagues to the Right

Some Days after, the King, being arrived at the Entrance of the Foreft, perceived the Fault of *Lager-Crona*. But fuppofing that he fhould fomewhere find a Way out, he followed the right Road, which led towards *Poczop*, not without a Thoufand Difficulties, being obliged to ftop every Moment, to make Bridges, and fell the Trees that blocked up the Way. Ten moft laborious and fatiguing Days March entirely ruined the Cavalry, and the greateft Part of the Baggage was fwallowed up. The Horfes had nothing to live on but the Leaves of Trees, nor the Men but a little Bifcuit and Roots.

When they came out of the Foreft, three Hundred Horfe of the firft Regiment of Cavalry were commanded to feize the faid Paffage of *Poczop*. But the *Mufcovites*, perceiving the King's Defign, prevented us, and detached a large Body of their Army, who floated all the Country, and fecured the Fidelity of the Inhabitants.

The King, feeing himfelf under a Neceffity of giving his Army Reft, and being willing to wait for News of General *Lager-Crona*, made a Halt for fifteen Days at the firft Villages he met in his Way, in which his Men found a great Abundance of Grain, and Plenty of Cattle, but not a fingle Man; the *Mufcovites* driving away the Inhabitants of all Places through which the *Swedes* were to march.

The

The Author fpeaks of Propofitions of Peace,
* made by the *Czar*: But it was wh,!e the King
was yet in *Saxony*, that a *French* Officer, named
Morel de Carriere, a Colonel in the Czar's Service,
made the Propofitions he fpeaks of ; offering the
Swedifh Monarch all Satisfaction, except that the
Czar would keep *Petersburgh* and *Wiburgh*. The
King would have accepted thefe Propofitions, on
Condition that *Petersburgh* fhould be entirely
razed, becaufe he had in reality a Defign to lend
France a Hand, when the Time of his Promife
made to the King of *England* was expired. But
the Czar, having in view the Eftablifhment of a
Marine , and the King, on his Part, feeing the
Danger of that Eftablifhment, and that the Czar,
who could build Ships with much more Facility than himfelf, would become Mafter of the
Baltic Sea, and render his Navy fuperior to
that of *Sweden*, he could never confent to leave
in his Hand thofe two Places which I have juft
now mentioned.

M *de Voltaire*'s Text
Amfterdam Edition, p. 239, &c *Englifh* Tranflation, p. 147.

Levenhaupt, *after having fuftained five Battles
againft fifty Thoufand Enemies, fwam over the* Soffa,
*followed by the five Thoufand Men he had left alive,
of whom the Wounded were carried over on Floats.
The Czar loft above twenty Thouf id Men in thefe
five Engagements, in which he had the Glory of
conquering the* Swedes, *and L. venhaupt the Reputation of difputing the Victory, and of retreating without being broken at laft. He then came to his Mafter's*
Çamp, &c.

REMARK.

THERE might be a great many Observations made in the Interval between the laſt Remark and this : But, as they are not of any great Conſequence, we paſs them over, to come to General *Levenhaupt*, who, after his Action with the Czar, falling into the Foreſt upon *Lager-Crona*'s Rout, followed and came up with him.

The King at laſt had ſome Tidings of *Lager-Crona*, and march'd to join him, being always engaged with the Enemy in ſlight Skirmiſhes, without any deciſive Action

M. *de Voltaire*'s Text.

Amſterdam Edition, p. 239, 240—246. *Engliſh* Tranſlation, p 152—158

The King of Sweden *ſaw himſel thus without Proviſions, his Communication with* Poland *cut off by Enemies who ſurrounded him, in the midſt of a Country where he had no Reſource but his Courage. In this Extremity, he did not aſſemble a Council of War, as many Relations have given out ; but, in the Night between the 7th and 8th of* July, *he ſent for Field Marſhal* Renchild *into his Tent, and ordered him, without Deliberation, and without Uneaſineſs, to prepare to attack the Czar the next Morning.* Renchild *did not diſpute his Maſter's Will, but went out with a Reſolution to obey him.* Then follows the Deſcription of the Battle, which may be read in the Author.

REMARK.

IN this Manner they found themſelves advanced into the Enemy's Country. The ſmall Cities and Villages being pretty diſtant from one another, it was neceſſary a little to extend the Quarters,

ters, in order to fubfift the Troops. General
Daldorf, with two Regiments of Foot, was at
Hadziacz, above fix *German* Leagues from the
reft of the Army. The *Mufcovites*, thinking to
furprize and carry him off, advanced by very long
Stages ; and the *King*, without reflecting on the
exceffive Cold, marched to fupport him. This
March very much ruined his Army. During
three whole Days in which they were expofed to
the Inclemency of the Weather, not only the
Men, but the Horfes, the Cattle, and even Birds,
died with Cold. The Soldiers, however, did not
want either Coats or Hofe, as fome Body has
made our Author believe.

The Day that the King was wounded, the
Mufcovites began to pafs the River *Worskla*, two
Leagues off of *Pultowa*. There Field-Marfhal
Reinfchild committed an unpardonable Fault For,
having all his Cavalry ringed in order of Battle,
nothing was more eafy than for him to cut off the
Enemies in the River, in proportion as they came
over ; whereas, without ftriking a Stroke, he
let them pafs, and intrench themfelves up to the
Chin. All the Reafon he gave for this was, that
he was unwilling to run any Hazard, for fear of
expofing the King's Perfon ; and that he thought
it the fafeft Way to draw up the Troops, and cover
his Majefty's Quarters.

The King was very angry at the fuperfluous and
ill-timed Precautions of the Field-Marfhal , but,
not being able himfelf to examine the Situation of
the Ground, nor to make any Difpofition there-
on, he was obliged to leave all to his General.

In the mean Time the *Mufcovites* intrenched
themfelves ; and advancing by Degrees, hemm'd
us in with Lines and Redoubts, continuing to do
fo for feven Days. The King, though very ill

of

of his Wound, had Word brought him of the State of Things ; and not thinking it proper to be blocked up by the Enemies under the Cannon of their Fortreſs, determined with himſelf that it was neceſſary to give Battle, and attack the E-nemy, without waiting to be attacked by them. His Orders were given the ſame Evening, and the whole Diſpoſition made.

Two thouſand Men guarded the Trench, twelve hundred Dragoons were with the Baggage. Thoſe who had been detached three, four, or five Leagues off, to procure Proviſions for the Army, amounting to about fifteen hundred Horſe, con-tinued where they were. Field-Marſhal *Reinſ-child*, who was divided a League from the gene-ral Quarters, was to be ready a Quarter of an Hour before Day, at the right Wing of the E-nemies, to fall on their Flank, at the ſame Time that the Infantry attacked them in Front. Four and twenty Men were ordered to carry the King in his Litter, that they might relieve one another.

Three Hours before Day, the King marched with his Infantry, and finding himſelf at firſt Dawn of Day preciſely within Muſket-Shot be-fore the Enemies Lines, who were at work with all Diligence, he attacked them, and forced ſeve-ral Redoubts at the Head of thoſe Lines. After an Action of above an Hour, not without very great Loſs, the Enemies gave Way, and began to retire, and the *Swedes* to purſue them.

The *Swediſh* Cavalry, having miſtook their Way in the Night, did not come up till after the Enemies had given Way.

Now there happened another Misfortune. Ma-jor-General *Roos* remained upon the Field of Battle, with ſix Battalions, to keep Poſſeſſion of ſeveral Redoubts which the Enemies had abandon-ed, and in which there were ſome Cannon. In
the

the mean Time, the Field-Marſhal *Reinſchild* rode up, and made the Infantry halt, to give Time for General *Roos* to rejoin the Army. The Cavalry, which had not yet been engaged, kept, as it had marched, in Columns, making the ſecond Line. This unfortunate Halt occaſioned the E-nemies to halt too, and give them Time to reco-ver from the Diſorder in which they had retreated towards the River, to repaſs it When they came to themſelves, and found they were purſued but by a Handful of Men, in Proportion to their own numerous Troops, they began to form themſelves, and range in Order of Battle, and to put themſelves in Motion towards the *Swedes.*

The King, heartily vexed to ſee the Battle in-terrupted, when it was already more than half gained, and obſerving the Motion of the Ene-mies, ſent, Time after Time, to the Field-Marſhal, to demand the Reaſon why he conti-nued ſo ſtill, while the Enemies advanced on them ? But this General, who on other Occaſions had ſhewn both Prudence and Valour, was ſo at a Loſs here, that he did nothing but run from one Side to the other, without giving one necef-ſary Order. He came at laſt up to the King, to tell him that the Enemies advanced, and that he was going to attack them ; to which the King anſwered, that ‘ it being impoſſible for him to ‘ act himſelf, he left him at Liberty to do what ‘ he thought proper. But, added he, the Loſs ‘ of Time does us a great Prejudice ’ Upon this the Field-Marſhal left the King, and made the Infantry wheel about to the Right, in order to face the Enemy, whom he advanced to attack, without ranging his Cavalry on his Wings to extend his Line, and hinder their falling upon him in Flank.

The

The *Mufcovites*, taking the Advantage of the *Swedifh* General's wrong Difpofition. through Means of that recovered the Day ; and, after one or two Difcharges, intirely furrounded the *Swedifh* Infantry, leaving the Horfe to ftraggle to the Right and Left in Diforder.

In the Attack of the Enemies Lines and Redoubts, the Litter, in which the King was carried, was both fhattered and repaired again under their Fire. Of the twenty-four Men who were felected to carry it, only three were left alive, and they were obliged to put two Horfes in their Room. The King all the while followed the Order of the Battle, and was often at the Head or in the Midft of the Battalions When the Action was renewed, and the Infantry were all hemmed in, his Majefty was in the fame Situation as the reft.

I leave to the Author the reft of the Relation of the Battle, and will only remark, that the *Swedes*, in this Action, did not amount to above fourteen thoufand Men, exclufive of thofe who remained in the Trenches, with the Baggage, &c. The Czar had above fourfcore thoufand of regular Troops, with a Train of a hundred and fifty Pieces of Cannon ; whereas the *Swedifh* Artillery was with the Baggage, they having no Ammunition to fupply it.

The King of *Sweden*'s Retreat towards the *Borifthenes* was not fo precipitate as has been pretended. Thofe who efcaped from the Battle with his Majefty, the Detachment that guarded the Baggage, the Train of Artillery, and moft of the Country People who had furnifhed his Army with Provifions, compofed this Retreat. Their firft March was only two Leagues, to *Schandarow*, where lay *Meyerfeldt*'s Regiment of Dragoons, to form a Magazine of Provifions. Here they refted all

all Night, and the next Day marched only three
Leagues to *Bielki*, to pick up five hundred Dragoons, commanded by Lieutenant-Colonel *Funk*,
who had been also detached in order to get in Provisions   They had two Days March more to the
Borysthenes, which they made pretty much at their
Ease, and without any great Hurry ; so that the
King did not arrive on the Banks of that River
till the fourth Day after the Loss of the Battle. It
was there that the greatest Part of the *Swedish* Cavalry came up with us.

The real Cause and Ground of this slow March,
was, amongst other Things, the King's Magnanimity; which induced him to give Time to the
Country People, who were with his Baggage on
the Day of the Battle, to retire by Degrees, to
cover them as he went along, and prevent their
falling into the Hands of the *Muscovites*.

When they were on the Bank of the *Boristhenes*,
the King got Information from *Mazeppa*, which
was the Road that led towards the *Crimea*, and
which went to *Bender* ; and was in some Doubt
which of them to chuse.

His Inclination was to take the former, in order to rest his Troops, and because there was
only one small River to cross that Way: But
Mazeppa's Advice determined him for the other.
As he pretended to know the Country, and computed only five Days Journey across the Desart,
before they arrived on the Frontiers of *Poland*,
this made the King alter his Intention, and resolve
to take that Route.   But, as all could not pass the
Boristhenes, they having but one Boat made of a
hollowed Tree, the first Care was to convey over
the King, *Mazeppa*, and his Escorte of three
hundred Horse, the Wounded, and the rest of
the Drabans. The King made *Mazeppa*'s Cossacks
pass over first.

E   As

As for the Cavalry, and the reſt of the Men eſcaped from the Battle, it was the King's Deſign to ſend them towards the *Crimea*. He ordered before him the two Generals *Levenhaupt* and *Kreutz*, and told the firſt, that he muſt follow him, as a Man proper for any Service, and therefore very neceſſary in their preſent Situation ; that he knew his great Capacity, either for War or for the Cabinet. To *Kreutz* he left the Conduct of all thoſe who could not paſs the *Boriſthenes*, with Orders to march towards the *Crimea* ; to carry with him all the Cheſts of Money, in order to ſubſiſt the Troops among the *Tartars* ; to burn the Carriages, and to throw the Cannon into the River.

He choſe to give this Command to General *Kreutz*, becauſe, beſides his Valour, which his Majeſty well knew, he was ſure in him of a blind Obedience to his Will, and that he would follow his Orders exactly according to the Letter.

But Count *Levenhaupt*, having ſo many gallant Actions before his Eyes, and having had the good Fortune to beat the *Muſcovites* ſeveral Times, ſolliciled warmly that his Majeſty would confer on him this Command. The King could not refuſe his Requeſt, and ſo left theſe two Generals with the Cavalry, and the other Remains of the Army.

M. *de Voltaire*'s Text.

Amſterdam Edition, p. 261. *Engliſh* Tranſlation, p. 161.

While the ſhattered Remains of the Army were in this Extremity, Prince Menzikoff *came up with ten thouſand Horſe, having each a Foot-Soldier be hind him.—The Prince ſent a Trumpet to the* Swe diſh *General, to offer him a Capitulation. Four General Officers were immediately ſent by* Leven
haupt

haupt, *to receive the Laws of the Conqueror.—The Capitulation was settled, and this whole Army were made Prisoners of War. Some of the Soldiers, grown desperate at their falling into the Hands of the* Muscovites, *threw themselves into the* Boristhenes. *Two Officers of* Troutfetre's *Regiment killed themselves upon the Spot. The rest were made Slaves.*

REMARK.

SCARCE had the King passed the River, before Prince *Menzikoff* appeared at the Head of fifteen thousand Men, with a great Sound of Drums, Kettle-Drums, and Trumpets, willing to have it thought, that the whole *Muscovite* Army was in pursuit of the Vanquished. He immediately sent a Summons to the *Swedish* General, requiring him to surrender at Discretion; ordering him to be told, that the Czar his Master was arrived, with all his victorious Troops; that he had it in his Option either to perish or submit; and that, if he did the latter, they might perhaps shew him some Favour.

If *Levenhaupt* had been informed of the Number of the Enemies, he would without Doubt have given them Battle: But, contrary to the common Rule and Custom among the *Swedes*, he called together the Colonels and Officers of superior Rank, to hold a Council of War upon the Course they had to take. The Opinions were divided: Some were for fighting, others for capitulating; and the Plurality of these latter carried it.

General *Kreutz* was sent to the Camp of the *Muscovites*, to conclude the Articles of Capitulation. When he appeared before *Menzikoff*, and saw that the whole Army was not there, he consented at once to all that the *Muscovite* General

demanded.

demanded. But, his Eagerneſs to return to his Troops, and the Facility with which he ſet his Hand to every Thing, occaſioned ſome Reflections in the Mind of a raſcally *Swediſh* Captive, who was in Prince *Menzikoff*'s Train. He remonſtrated to the Prince, that *Kreutz*, inſtead of ſtanding to the Capitulation, would cauſe the Troops to advance ; and that the *Ruſſians* would be infallibly beaten, as they were not ſtrong enough to oppoſe the *Swediſh* Cavalry, which had never yet been engaged. Theſe Reflections prevailed on *Menzikoff* to retain General *Kreutz*, and ſend Officers of his own to *Levenhaupt*, who cofcluded the Articles of his Capitulation, and his Captivity.

M. *de Voltaire*'s Text.
Amſterdam Edition, p 266, & *ſeq*. *Engliſh* Tranſlation, p. 164, 165.

Charles XII *had loſt in one Day the Fruit of nine Years Pains, and almoſt a hundred Battles. He fled in a wretched Calaſh—acroſs a Deſart, where they found neither Huts, Tents, Men, Animals, nor Roads. Every thing was wanting there, even to Water itſelf. 'Twas then the Beginning of* July: *The Country is ſituated in the* 47th *Degree. The dry Sand in the Deſart made the Heat of the Sun the more inſupportable. The Horſes fell by the Way, and the Men were ready to die with Thirſt.* Count Poniatowſki, *who was a little better mounted than the reſt, advanced before them into the Plains, and having ſpied a Willow, he judged there muſt be Water nigh. He ſearched about till he found the Spring. This happy Diſcovery ſaved the Lives of the King of* Sweden's *little Troop.*

R E-

R E M A R K.

WHILE *Levenhaupt* was capitulating, the King, perfuaded that his General was retiring towards the *Crimea*, rode away from the River, and marched the reft of the Day, and all the Night, under the Guidance of *Mazeppa*'s People.

Prince *Menzikoff* fent General *Wolkonski*, with fix Thoufand Men, in purfuit of him. *Wolkonski* made his Horfes, as the *Swedes* had done, fwim over the River, and ufed the fame Boat as they did for himfelf and his Men.

As it was late before he got over all his People he followed the Track of a fick Officer's Calafh and fo loft the Route that the King had taken. When he came up with this unhappy Officer, he revenged on him his own Miftake. But this Hindrance and Lofs of Time was advantageous to the King in his Retreat, which he continued without ftopping all the next Day.

This March was by fo much the more fatiguing, as the Guides, having loft the Pofition of the Place, and not being able to find the Eaft, did not know themfelves where abouts they were, in the midft of a Defart where both Men and Horfes were ready to die with Thirft.

Count *Poniatowski, &c.* as the Author has related.

M. *de Voltaire*'s Text.
Amfterdam Edition, p. 267, & *feq. Englifh* Tranflation, p 165, 166.

*After five Days March the King found himfelf upon the Banks of the—*Bogh*—on the other Side of which is the little City of* Oczakow, *a Frontier of the* Turkifh *Empire.* —— *The King fent to demand a Paffage over.* —— *In the mean Time the* Mufcovites,
after

after having paffed the Borifthenes, *purfued the King with all poffible Speed.* He had *fcarce paffed the* Bogh *in the* Turkifh *Boats, before his Enemies appeared, to the Number of almoft fix Thoufand Horfemen*; *and his Majefty had the Misfortune to fee five Hundred of his little Troop, who had not been able to get over time enough, feized by the* Mufcovites *on the other Side of the River.* The Bafhaw *of* Oczakow *asked his Pardon for the Delays, which had occafioned the taking of thefe five Hundred Men Prifoners.* — The Commander of Bender — *fent an Aga to compliment the King, and to offer him* — *the Conveniences requifite to conduct him with Magnificence to* Bender.

REMARK.

AFTER three Days March, it was perceived that the Paffage of the River *Hippanis*, at this Day the *Bogh*, was impracticable in the Defart ; they having no Boats, nor the Means of making any ; befides that they muft have ftarved while they were about it. *Mazeppa*'s Opinion was, that the King fhould make the beft of his way towards *Oczakow*, where, being fuccoured and affifted by his pretended Friend the Bafhaw of the Place, as he expected, they might furmount the Difficulty of the Paffage. It was refolved to follow this Advice.

The King employed Count *Poniatowski* to go with all Expedition to *Oczakow*, in order to remove, with the Bafhaw, all the Obftacles that might lie in their Way, and to prepare every Thing for his Majefty's Paffage. *Poniatowski*, having furnifhed himfelf with Guides, rode full Speed towards the Banks of the *Bogh*, at the Place where that River falls into the *Black Sea* ; but he could fee neither *Oczakow*, nor any Means of paffing over.

At

At laft, after riding and looking almoft all Day, he difcovered on the Sea-fhore five Men gathering of Salt. But thefe Fellows, when they faw Men on Horfeback coming towards them, got into their Boat, and put out to Sea.

After having called after them a long Time, and ufed abundance of Intreaties, fhewing them Money, he prevailed upon them at laft to come to Shore, and treated with them for a Paffage over the River, on the other Side of which he could fee fome People got together, without diftinguifhing what they were, the River being very broad at that Place.

The Boatmen had Arms with them, and looked very much like Highwaymen. Thofe on the other Side were *Turkifh* Slaves, who were hewing Stone for the Fortifications of *Oczakow*.

When *Poniatowfki* got over, without his Horfe, he found he had four *German* Leagues to *Oczakow*. It was very fortunate that he had with him a *Tartar*, who fpoke *French*. By Means of this Man, after a Thoufand Difficulties, he found a Horfe, and rode to *Oczakow* on a full Gallop before Night.

He was ftopp'd in the Suburbs by the *Turkifh* Guard ; and in fpite of all his Reprefentations of the Neceffity he was under of fpeaking to the Bafhaw, he was obliged to pafs the Night with Impatience, and to wait till nine o' Clock in the Morning for the getting-up of this *Turkifh* Lord, who at laft came into a Garden without the Town to give him Audience.

The Count did all in his Power, to perfuade this Governor to let him have Boats for bringing over the King. But, feeing his Rhetorick had no Effect, he had recourfe to folid Arguments ; and, by the Mediation of two Thoufand Ducats, which

which he gave him upon the Spot, the Bashaw became more flexible, and Perfuasion began to take Place.

They agreed that the *Turks* fhould fend over five Barks with Provifions; that the *Swedes* fhould buy thofe Provifions; and that, at the fame Time, they fhould bring back with them the King and his Retinue.

As foon as this Convention began to be put in Execution, and *Poniatowski* faw the Barks fet fail, he made all Hafte to inform the King of it, and repaffed the River in the Place where his Boat waited for him. He found his Majefty juft arrived on the other Side of the River, and gave him much Pleafure with his Relation.

One of the five Barks foon arrived, and its Cargo was fold for almoft the Weight in Gold. But inftead of pufhing a-fhore to take any Body in, the Men immediately put out again towards the Middle. The others would have done the fame; but the *Swedes* feized them by force, put the *Turks* fairly on fhore, and began to pafs over juft as *Wolkonski* arrived, who found three Hundred *Swedes* and *Coffacks* left behind, and made them Prifoners. The King himfelf had been taken, if he had ftaid an Hour longer.

The Governor of *Oczakow* came to meet the King, and prayed his Majefty to advance near the City, that he might be better furnifhed with Conveniences. The King did fo, and refted there one Day.

Here a *Turkifh* Officer of the Houfhold of *Juf fuff*, Bafhaw-Seraskier of *Bender*, came to compliment the King in the Name of the Seraskier; offered him fome Refrefhments, with a fmall Tent to fleep in, and invited his Majefty to pafs on to *Bender*, where he would be better fituated than at *Oczakow*. The King accepted his Offers, ordered

ordered a Thousand Ducats to be given him for his Pains, and took the Road of *Bender*.

The Seraskier's Attention to procure all manner of Conveniences for the King, was extraordinary. They found on the Road Chariots and Horses to be lett. Every Station was a kind of Market, where all Sorts of Provisions, Clothes, &c. were sold ; with Orders not to exact an excessive Price, and to take such Money as they had.

At the Distance of two Days Journey from *Oczakow*, there came a Man to compliment the King from the Kan of the *Tartars*, bringing with him Refreshments, and a fine embroidered Tent. The Han's Emissary was entertained in the same Manner as the Bashaw's. At the Distance of one Days Journey from *Bender*, three Hundred of the Seraskier's Light-Horse came to meet the King, and to escort him.

When his Majesty arrived at the Banks of the *Niester*, which runs by *Bender*, he was saluted by all the Artillery of the Castle. The Seraskier, at the Head of his Garrison, came over the *Niester* on Foot, desired the King to alight, and received his Majesty in a superb Tent, which he offered him to repose in.

The next Day he brought the Keys of the City, and the Castle ; inviting his Majesty to take up his Residence there, and to give his Orders, which should be absolutely obey'd. In a Word, never was there seen a *Turk* more open, more polite, and more diligent. The King, at his Persuasion, crossed the River, and took up his Camp under the Cannon of the Fortress, without accepting the Bashaw's Offer of Lodging in the Castle itself.

The Bashaw then regulated, with the Intendant of the King's Houshold, the Expence for

F   the

the Maintenance of his Retinue, and ordered five Hundred Crowns *per* Day to be iffued, to fupply them with Provifions. All this was done without Order from the Porte, which however approved of the Bafhaw's whole Proceeding.

This good old Man made his Appearance regularly, every other Day, in the King's Tent, to be informed of his Majefty's Health.

The Garrifon was moft rigoroufly forbid to infult the *Swedes*, and a fevere Order was iffued to avoid all Sorts of Quarrels. If any ever happened, the *Turks* were always to blame.

Five Hundred *Janiffaries* guarded the King's Camp. The Regularity of his Life, the Simplicity of his Drefs, his Abftinence from Wine and Women, a Devotion without Oftentation, publick Prayers twice a Day regularly, attracted the Admiration of the *Turks*, and made his Majefty much revered.

When he was cured of his Wound, and began to take the Air in his Camp, and in that of the *Janiffaries* who were ordered for his Guard, one of them came up to him with a little too much Familiarity, clapped him on the Shoulder, and faid aloud, ' Why has not Heaven given us fuch a Mafter ? We fhould then conquer all the World.'

As foon as he arrived in the *Turkifh* Territories, the King immediately refolved to fend a Perfon to *Conftantinople*, to thank the Grand Signior for the good Reception he had met with, and the great Good-Manners that were fhewn him in his Dominions. But the little Knowledge that the *Swedes* had of the *Turks*, was the Reafon that no Man would take upon him that Commiffion.

There

There was found in the King's Retinue, a *Dantzicker*, whose Name was Mr. *Neugebaver*. He had been formerly Preceptor to the young Czarewitz, but had left *Ruſſia* without asking Leave. Uneaſy on account of his Situation, dreading to fall into the Hands of the *Muſcovites*, and ſolliciting the King continually for Leave to go to *Conſtantinople*, where he might embark for *Holland*, he offered to take charge of the King's Letter to the Grand Signior, and was immediately diſpatched with it.

Upon his Arrival at *Conſtantinople*, he demanded of the Grand Viſir to be introduced to the Sultan, in order to deliver to him the King his Maſter's Letter, as he had undertaken. The Viſir required it himſelf ; telling him, that no Man could ever appear before the Grand Signior, without a publick Character. The Sieur *Neugebaver* continued to inſiſt, on his part, that he would abſolutely deliver this Letter into the Grand Signior's own Hands, becauſe the King his Maſter had commanded him ſo to do ; but his Repreſentation had no Effect.

The Baſhaw of *Bender*, being informed of the Difficulty that hindered the Admiſſion of M. *Neugebaver*, intreated the King ſo earneſtly to ſend him a Character, that his Majeſty conſented to it, and immediately ordered an Inſtrument, conſtituting him his Envoy Extraordinary.

Count *Poniatowſki*, having the Curioſity to ſee the Grand Signior's Court, and the Capital of the Eaſt, aſked the King's Permiſſion for ſix Weeks, and offered at the ſame Time to carry the Expreſs to the Sieur *Neugebaver*, that he might thus have an Opportunity of ſeeing the Ceremony of an Audience. His Majeſty gave him leave, on Condition that he ſhould come back at the Time appointed ; becauſe he flattered himſelf, that, in

this

this Interval, his Wound would heal, and he should have some News from the King of *Poland*, who had remained in that Kingdom with a Body of ten thouland *Swedes*, under the Command of General *Craffau*, and whom he intended to join when he knew where he lay

Besides the Dispatch for M. *Neugebaver*, Count *Poniatowski* was charged with a Letter of Compliment from the King to the Grand Vizir; in order to procure him an Opportunity to see that Prime Minister of the *Ottoman* Empire.

The Grand Visir took Pleasure in questioning Count *Poniatowski* concerning the different Actions of the King of *Sweden* against the *Muscovites*, concerning the Forces of *Sweden* by Sea and Land, and whatever else regarded that Nation. He had by his Side a Sea-Captain, a *Swede* by Birth, but a Renegade, in order to know, as it seemed, if Count *Pomatowski*'s Relation and Answers were conformable to Truth, and if they agreed with what the Captain had told him. Finding it to be so, he said in *Turkish*, ' This ' Heathen does not know how to lye.'

At the Conclusion of a very long Audience, *Poniatowski* asked Leave of the Grand Visir to see all the Curiofities of *Constantinople*, the Treafuries, the Palaces, the Mofques, and, in a Word, every Thing that was to be seen. The Vifir told him, that even Ambassadors themselves did not enjoy that Privilege. Upon that Count *Poniatowski* immediately demanded the *Ferman*, that is, an Order for the Post, that he might return, since he could have nothing more to tell the King, except he had seen the City and the Marine. The Visir smiled at this, and ordered a Gentleman of the Court to accompany the Count wherever he had a Mind to go, and to let him see all that he desired.

This

This Beginning, and such a favourable Recep-, tion of a Stranger, contrary to all *Turkish* Custom, very much surprised every Body. All the Doors were opened to him, and nothing escaped his Curiosity. He rewarded all those liberally who took the Pains to shew him what he wanted to see. This furnished him with useful Informations, and acquired him particular Regard.

In the mean time M. *Neugebaver* had his Audience of the Grand Signior, at which Count *Poniatowski* was present. That being over, he demanded the *Ferman* for his Return. The Grand Visir made him come to his Palace; and asked him with great Politeness, ' Why he was in such ' Haste to leave *Constantinople* ?' Adding, ' that ' they saw him there with Pleasure, and that he ' must continue longer among them.' *Poniatowski* laid before him his Master's Orders; told him the Time of his Permission was already expired; that he must return at the Day appointed, for fear of incurring his Majesty's Displeasure; and that, unless he was detained by Force, he could not stay any longer at *Constantinople*. The Visir then told him, that since he knew not how to make him stay, he should have the *Ferman* in three Days; but, that he should be glad to speak with him again before his Departure, and to see him dressed as he was when he went through the Streets of *Constantinople*, to view the Curiosities.

On the Day of his Departure, *Poniatowski*, in a *Turkish* Dress, waited upon the Visir, who expressed his Pleasure at the Sight. After much Conversation, the Visir charged him to assure the King of the Grand Signior's perfect Friendship, and of the particular Attachment which he himself had for his royal Person . That he prayed his Majesty not to be in Haste to depart, nor to

expose

expofe his Perfon to any Danger: That the Grand Signior had refolved to have him conducted quite to his own Dominions, by what Way he fhould chufe himfelf, with an Efcorte fufficient for the Security of his Perfon: That the King's Friendfhip was precious to his Highnefs, who was defirous to preferve it.

When Count *Poniatowski* would have got up to take Leave, he made him fit down again, and ordered him to be prefented with a large Purfe full of Gold; telling him, that he knew the Liberalities he had fhewn all over *Conftantinople*, and that he was not willing to let him want Money on the Road. *Poniatowski* thanked the Vifir for his Care and Generofity, but refufed to take the Purfe The Interpreter to the *Porte*, *Mauro Cordato*, who was afterwards Hofpodar of *Walachia*, endeavoured to perfuade the Count to accept the Offer; telling him, that his Refufal would offend the Grand Vifir: But he anfwered, that Men of a certain Rank, who had the Honour to be near the Perfons of Kings, never took Prefents from any one whatfoever, except their own Mafters.

The Vifir wanted to know what they were contending about, and the Interpreter was afraid to tell him. At laft the Minifter commanded it, and being informed, ordered him to tell *Poniatowski*, that the Prefent came from the Grand Signior himfelf. The Count then took the Purfe; declaring, that he looked upon it as a very fingular Grace from his Highnefs. At the fame Time he took leave of the Vifir, made fome Prefents to that Minifter's Domefticks, and fet out immediately for *Bender*.

M. *de Voltaire*'s Text.
Amfterdam Edition, p. 274--276. *Englifh* Tranflation, p. 169, 170.

*To the moft high, moft glorious, invincible, and
auguft Emperor of many Empires, King of many
Kingdoms, Head and Protector of many Nations;
may the Almighty blefs and prolong your Reign!
We give Advice to your Imperial Highnefs, &c.*

Charles XII,
Son of Charles XI.

R E M A R K.

THE King of *Sweden*'s Letter never had
any fuch Senfe as is here given to it. It
contained merely the King's Thanks to the Grand
Signior for the good Reception he had met with
in his Dominions, and fpoke of nothing elfe.

That Prince, the fworn Enemy of all Flattery,
never figned a Letter fo full of Vanity and Oftentation.

As he had fimply figned, at the Bottom of his
Letter, *your good Brother and Friend,* juft as if
he had writ to a Chriftian Prince, that Subfcrip-
tion made much Impreffion upon the Grand Signior's Mind, and had a very good Effect for the
King of *Sweden.*

M. *de Voltaire*'s Text.
Amfterdam Edition, p 278. *Englifh* Tranflation, p 171.

Count Poniatowfki, *a Man equally capable and
refolute, infinuating and fupple, born with the Ta-
lent of perfuading and pleafing all Nations, attend-
ed the* Swedifh *Embaffy, but in a private Capacity,
in order to found the Difpofitions of the* Conftantino-
politan *Minifter, without being tied up to the ufual
Forms, and giving too much Ground for Sufpicion.*

R E-

REMARK.

COUNT *Poniatowski's* firſt Journey to. *Conſtantinople*, as has been already obſerved, was only out of mere Curioſity. But, as the Grand Viſir had, at his Departure, by Order of the Grand Signior, made by him ſeveral conſiderable Advances to the King of *Sweden*, with Promiſes of Aſſiſtance, an Eſcort, and a real Support, and as the ſame Viſir, being won over by the Czar, began to fail of what he had promiſed ; Count *Poniatowski* had Orders to repair to *Conſtantinople*, and to labour at his Depoſition.

M. *de Voltaire's* Text.

Amſterdam Edition, p. 279. *Engliſh* Tranſlation, 172.

Poniatowski *entered into cloſe Friendſhip with one* Bru, *a* Frenchman, *who had been Chancellor to the* French *Embaſſy.*

REMARK.

IT was an old *Hungarian* Gentleman, named *Ferens Houat*, a Refugee at *Conſtantinople*, and perfectly well acquainted with the Manners of the People, that *Poniatowski* entered into Friend-ſhip with.

M. *de Voltaire's* Text.

Amſterdam Edition, p. 280. *Engliſh* Tranſlation, p. 172.

One of thoſe who ſeconded Poniatowski's *Deſigns with the greateſt Abilities, was* Fonſeca, *a* Portu-gueſe *Phyſician and* Jew, *whom I knew very well at* Paris, *but who was then ſettled at* Con-ſtantinople.

R E-

R E M A R K.

It was not a *Jew*, but a *French* Renegade, the chief Surgeon of the Seraglio, by Name Mr. *Goin*.

M. *de Voltaire*'s Text.

Amsterdam Edition, p. 231. *English* Translation, p. 173.

The Grand Vifir — *said to* Poniatowski, *giving him a Purse with a Thousand Ducats, ' I will take your King in one Hand, and a Sword in the other, and conduct him to* Moscow *at the Head of two Hundred Thousand Men.'*

R E M A R K.

It was not the Vifir before mentioned who spoke thus to Count *Poniatowski*.

M. *de Voltaire*'s Text.

Amsterdam Edition, p. 288 — 314. *English* Translation, p. 177 — 194.

To dispose the Ottoman Porte *to this War (with the* Muscovites, Charles XII) *detached about eight Hundred* Poles *and* Coflicks *of his Retinue, with Orders to pass the* Niester, *that runs by* Bender, *and to go and observe what passed upon the Frontiers of* Poland. — *The* Muscovites — *fell immediately upon this little Company, and pursued them even to the Territories of the Grand Signior. This was what the King of* Sweden *expected. His Ministers and Emiffaries at the Porte made a great Clamour against this Irruption, and excited the* Turks *to Vengeance: But the* Czar's *Money furmounted all Difficulties.* Tolstoy, *his Envoy at* Constantinople, *gave the Grand Vifir, and his Creatures, Part of the six Millions that had been found at* Pultowa *in*

G   *the*

the King of Sweden*'s military Cheſt. After ſuch a*
a Defence, the Divan found the Czar not guilty.
— *They even granted to his Envoy ſuch Honours*
and Privileges as the Muſcovite *Miniſters had never*
before enjoy'd at Conſtantinople.——Charles *(thus)*
abandoned by the Grand Viſir, and conquered by the
Czar's Money in Turkey, *as he had been by his*
Arms in Ukrania, —— *believed that the Sultan*
was ignorant of the Intrigues of Chourlouly Ali
his Grand Viſir, reſolved to make him acquainted
with them, and Poniatowski *undertook this bold*
Commiſſion — *This old Miniſter, who had long*
and faithfully ſerved his Maſter —— *was de-*
prived of his Dignity, his Wealth, and his
Wife, Daughter of the laſt Sultan Muſtapha, *and*
baniſhed to Caffa — *in* Crim Tartary. *The Bull,*
that is to ſay, the Seal of the Empire was given to
Numan Cuprougli, *Grandſon to him who took*
Candia — *He was depoſed, after a Miniſtry of*
two Months. — *His rigid Probity, they ſay, was*
the ſole Cauſe of his Fall. — Achmet *reproaching*
him, that his Predeceſſor could find other Ways and
Means to pay the Troops, he anſwered ' *If he had*
the Art to enrich your Highneſs by Rapines, it is
ſuch an Art as I eſteem it an Honour to be ignorant
of' *His Freedom did not coſt him his Head* — *He*
had leave to retire into the Iſle of Negropont.'

R E M A R K.

AT the Return of Count *Poniatowski* to *Ben-*
der, after his firſt Journey to *Conſtantino-*
ple, the King of *Sweden*, charmed with his Relation, with the magnificent Promiſes of the
Grand Signior by the Mouth of Grand Viſir, and
the Aſſurances of that Miniſter, thought his Glory, his Intereſt, and the Support of King *Staniſ-*
laus upon the Throne of *Poland*, could not be
bet-

better provided for, than by a Power fo foimida-
ble as that of the *Ottoman* Empire.

But the News that the Grand Vifir, after all thefe
fine Declarations, had renewed the Peace with
the Czar, even after the Irruption of the *Mufcovites* into *Moldavia*, and the carrying-off three
Hundred *Swedes* in the Territories of the Grand
Signior, very much interrupted the Joy of
Charles XII.

A Mifunderftanding, that happened between
the *Swedifh* Envoy and the Grand Vifir, though
the Fault of the former, compleatly foured his
Majefty's Mind.

The firft Mark of Refentment that he fhewed
to the *Turkifh* Minifter, was to refufe his Prefents,
which he had fent along with thofe that came
from the Grand Signior himfelf. The fecond
was his fending back Count *Poniatowski* to Conftantinople, with Orders to try all Means to get
him depofed.

This Commiffion was far from being relifhed
by him who was charged with it; efpecially as
the Grand Vifir had before taken fo much Pains
to oblige him. But, to execute the King's
Will, it was neceffary to forget all the Refpect
and Civility that the Grand Vifir had fhewn
him; and even to hazard his Life over and
over.

The Grand Vifir, having broke off all Commerce with the Envoy *Neugebaver*, omitted nothing that might teftify his Regard to Count *Poniatowski*, upon his Arrival again at *Conftantinople*.
The Count, however, was to do his Duty. Such a
thorny Negociation required Abundance of Circumfpection, Time, and Intrigue. He fet every
Spring to work; and at laft fucceeded. The
Grand Vifir was depofed and ftrangled; and
Orders were given to make Preparations for

War,

War, without any formal Declaration. *Kou-prouli Numan* Bashaw, a close Friend of Count *Poniatowski*, was made Grand Visir.

This new Minister, whose Name is well known on account of the many Visirs of the same Family, who had performed very great Services to the *Ottoman* Empire, was a Man of most singular Probity. He loved Justice extremely, preferred it to all other Considerations, rendered it to all Mankind without Distinction, and even carried it sometimes to an Excess. To make his Character thoroughly known, I shall insert here some Circumstances that perhaps will give the Reader Pleasure.

He had been made Governor of *Erzerum*. When he went to take Possession of his Government, one of his Retinue used a poor Woman ill, and took from her a Pot of Milk, which was all she had to support her. The Woman complained of it to the Bashaw, with Tears in her Eyes. *Kou-prouli*, having asked her if she should know the Man again who had committed this Violence, ordered all his Domesticks to be called together. The Woman, seeing the guilty Person, pointed him out to the Bashaw : But, as the Fact had passed without Witnesses, the *Turk*, perceiving he could not be convicted, denied it absolutely. *Kouprouli* then exhorted the Woman to take Care, and speak the Truth ; for if she did not, she should herself suffer what he was now going to inflict on the Person accused. As she boldly assured him that she was not mistaken, he had the Fellow's Head struck off on the Spot ; and having ordered his Stomach to be opened, they found there the crude Milk, it not having yet undergone a Digestion. The Woman was rewarded with the Spoils of the Dead, and sent away in Peace.

When

When he was in his Office at *Erzerum*, under the Reign of Sultan *Muſtapha*, there was in his Government a *Turkiſh* Officer, a near Relation of the Mufti, who at that Time was the Grand Signior's chief Favourite The Buſineſs of this Officer was to raiſe the Impoſts on the People. Supported by the Credit of the Mufti, he often exerciſed his Power with crying Acts of Violence and Injuſtice, imagining that every Thing he did would be countenanced.

Having borrowed a Purſe of Money of an *Armenian*, upon his Note of Hand; when the Time ſpecified was elapſed, the Creditor demaned Payment: But all the Satisfaction he received, was by Way of Menace. He complained of this to the Baſhaw, who ordered the Debtor to pay the Money.

The Officer, enraged at the *Armenian*'s Audaciouſneſs, that he ſhould dare to complain, ordered five hundred Blows to be given him with a Cudgel, inſtead of five hundred Crowns; threatening, that if he complained any more, he ſhould have his Brains beat out. The poor *Armenian*, paid in this bad Coin, deplored in Secret his Drubbing and his Loſs, without any further Thoughts of demanding Juſtice.

Some Time after, the Baſhaw having met him in his Way, and perceiving that he ſhunned him, ſent a Meſſenger after him to enquire if he had been paid? The *Armenian* did not dare to ſay either Yes or No, for Fear of more ill Uſage, till the Baſhaw commanded him poſitively to tell the Truth. He did; and when *Kouprouli* heard how he had been treated, he ſent immediately and had the Debtor hung up at his own Door, and confiſcated all his Effects to the *Armenian*'s Profit.

The

The Mufti, having heard of his Relation's Death, accufed the Bafhaw of many Crimes, all of them falfe, and pronounced Sentence to have him ftrangled. A Capitzi was fent to *Erzerum*, to demand the Head of the Bafhaw, in the Name of the Grand Signior; a Demand, which no Man was ever known to oppofe. *Kouprouli* however refufed to obey fo unjuft an Order, and inftantly took the Refolution to go himfelf to *Conftantinople*, and make his Defence in full Divan. He did it with fo much Succefs, that his Difobedience was not adjuged to be criminal.

The Mufti, all in Confufion, referved his Rancour aguinft the Bafhaw *Numan* for another Opportunity; but, being maffacreed, in a fhort Time after, by the People of *Adrianople*, he had not the Satisfaction to fatiate his Vengeance.

This Mufti, having been Preceptor to Sultan *Muftapha* in his Youth, had got fo much the Afcendant over his Mind, that he governed him abfolutely when he came to be Emperor. He committed with Impunity all Sorts of Injuftices and Violences, and was the Caufe of his Mafter's Depofition, fo well known for an extraordinary Event.

Kouprouli had a Reputation fo well eftablifhed, that he was fent for to *Conftantinople* by Sultan *Achmet*, who had determined to give him his Niece in Marriage. After the nuptial Ceremony, the Sultana was fent home to her Husband's Houfe, with her Bridal Ornaments, and twelve Eunuchs for *Numan*'s Seraglio. But this Bafhaw fent back the Eunuchs to the Grand Signior. Every one judged from this Refufal, that he was inevitably loft: But, when he was asked the Reafon of what he had done, he anfwered with an extraordinary Greatnefs of Mind, 'That having married a free Princefs, he had no Occafion for
Eu-

Eunuchs to guard her: Whereas to the Grand Signior, who had only Slaves in his Seraglio, such
a Guard as that was neceſſary.'

All theſe Circumſtances ſhew the Genius, and
the elevated Sentiments of this great Man, Sentiments that are very uncommon under a *Turkiſh*
Government

He was no ſooner made Grand Viſir, but he
began to take Meaſures for the fulfilling the Engagements that had been entered into with the
King of *Sweden*, to whom the Grand Signior
ſent eight hundred Purſes, by way of Loan,
without requiring any Security whatſoever.

The Viſir ſent for *Tolſtoy*, the *Muſcovite* Ambaſſador, and told him, that he ought not to take
the leaſt Umbrage at the Preparations which he
ſaw carrying on at the *Porte*, that the only In-
tent of them was to conduct the King of *Sweden*,
their Gueſt, back to his Dominions thro' *Poland*;
but, that he ſhould proceed cautiouſly and ſe-
curely in that Affair, and would be glad to know
if the Czar would not oppoſe it.

The Ambaſſador replied, that his Maſter
having nothing to do in *Poland*, would not
oppoſe it there on his own Account: But, that
being in Alliance with the King of *Poland*, and
under an Obligation, by Treaties, to furniſh him
with forty thouſand well diſciplined Men, when-
ever he ſhould demand them, he believed the
King of *Poland* would make uſe of thoſe Troops
to hinder his Enemy's Paſſage thro' that Kingdom.

The Viſir then declared to him, that he would
march himſelf at the Head of the Eſcorte, and
that it ſhould conſiſt of an hundred thouſand
Men; ' and if, ſays he, I ſhould think more
would be neceſſary, I will as take many as there
Hairs in my Beard, clapping his Hand to his
Chin

Chin as he fpoke. ' We will pay for every Thing
as we pafs, we will treat Friends as Friends ; but
whoever fhall dare to oppofe us, we fhall immediately fall on them as Enemies.'

At the fame Time he fent for Count *Poniatowski*, and communicated to him his Converfation
with the *Mufcovite* Ambaffador: After which
every Thing feemed to be in Motion for an Expedition.

As he would have in the Troops only chofen
Men, and the Body of Janiffaries was commanded by an old Officer of very indifferent
Reputation, he fent into *Afia* for another Perfon, to put him in his Place. The old Man
having heard this, and being defirous to prevent
his own Difgrace, waited on the Grand Signior,
and told him, that, as the Grand Vifir's Father
had depofed his Highnefs's Father, the Son was
now contriving to do the fame by his Highnefs ;
that he was continually fhut up with Men of the
Law, to deliberate thereupon ; that he was a-
dored by the Populace, and even by the Janiffaries ; and that his Highnefs was not fure of fitting
a Moment longer on his Throne.

The Sultan intimidated, in this Manner, without
diftinguifhing Truth from Calumny, fent immediately for the Grand Vifir, and demanded back
the Seal. But, not daring to touch his Life, on
account of his great Credit, he faw him that
inftant put on board a Galley, and fent him to
Negropont, in Quality of Governor.

After the Depofition of *Kouprouli*, the Government of the City was given to one *Soliman*, a Bafhaw
of the Divan, with the Title of Kaimacan. He was a
Georgian by Nation, a Man of a very limited Underftanding, very covetous of Riches, and who afterwards fold himfelf to *Ruffia*. As he had not Authority enough to decide Affairs of State, every
Thing

Thing languished, and seemed to be neglected, without a Visiriate. This continued several Months

The Credit of Count *Poniatowski* was however very well established He neglected nothing that his Liberty of acting put in his Power, during this Interval, to keep the Grand Signior fixed in his Resolution of making War against the *Russians*.

All his Intrigues, and underhand Dealings, gave great Uneasiness to the *Muscovite* Minister, who, foreseeing that a War would be unavoidable, endeavoured to corrupt Count *Poniatowski*, who was the first Mover of every Thing. He offered him, in the Czar's Name, a hundred thousand Roubles, with the Post of General of the Artillery, and a considerable Estate in *Ukrania*. But seeing his Offers rejected, and his Labour lost, he tried another Expedient, to get him out of the Way; which was, to poison him.

One of his Domesticks was seduced into the Plot. They gave him the Poison in a small Phial, and payed him by way of Advance half his Recompence. But, by a particular Providence, the Phial was broke in his Hands, and they were obliged to provide another. In this Interval the Wretch, after some Reflections, repented of his wicked Design, and informed his Master of it, continuing still to pursue his Engagement with the *Muscovite* Ambassador's People, in order the better to unravel the Affair

When the second Poison was ready, M. *Tolstoy*, that he might not fail of his Purpose, joined a trusty Fellow of his own with Count *Poniatowski*'s Domestick He was with his own Hand to pour the Poison into the Cup, in which the Servant was to give Coffee to his Master *Poniatowski*. But, the Snares were so well laid, that the Birds were

H   taken,

taken, and fent to the Great Divan, in order to receive their due Sentence and Punifhment.

The Kaimacan did all in his Power to fave the Honour of the *Mufcovite* Ambaffador. He gave out that Count *Poniatowski's* Interpreter was a Calumniator, and treated the Delinquents, who confeffed the Fact, and accufed themfelves, as Liars and Impoftors. An *Afian* Judge, being prefent at the Divan, and feeing fo much Partiality, told the Kaimacan, that they could not difpenfe with doing Juftice to all the Parties ; and that they muft hear every body, and examine the Fact to the Bottom. He then ordered a Dog to be brought, and made him fwallow fome of the Poifon in Milk. The Dog burft in half an Hour after ; and they could no longer doubt of the Truth of what had been depofed. M. *Tolftoy's* Domeftick, who was engaged in the Affair, they condemned for five Years to the Gallies, where he died a Year after : But Count *Poniatowski's* Servant, who, after he had repented of his ill Defign, had informed his Mafter of it, was fet at Liberty.

Count *Poniatowski*, not fatisfied with this Decree, reprefented very warmly the Confequences of fuch a Procedure, and the little Safety there was for Minifters who were juftly and honourably inclined. He infifted, that they fhould fend home *Tolftoy*, as unworthy of the Place he filled, and require another Ambaffador in his Place. The Mufti, a particular Friend of *Poniatowski*, appeafed him ; promifing, that in a fhort Time, there fhould be no Need either of *Tolftoy*, or of any other in his Room ; and that they only waited the Arrival of him who was defigned for the Vifiriate.

Mr. *de Voltaire*'s Text.
Amsterdam Edition, p. 314, *&c.* *English* Transflation, p. 194.

After this the Grand Signior sent to Aleppo *for* Baltagi Mehemet, *Bashaw of* Syria, *who had been Grand Visir before* Chourlouly.—*At the Time that this* Mehemet *was a Servant in the Seraglio, he had the good Fortune to do Prince* Achmet *some small Piece of Service, that Prince being then a Prisoner of State in the Reign of his Brother* Muftapha.--- Achmet, *upon his becoming Sultan, gave one of his Slaves, whom he had loved very much, to* Baltagi Mehemet. *This Woman, by her Intrigues, made her Husband Grand Visir. Another Intrigue depofed him, and a third made him Visir again.*

REMARK.

THE History of *Baltad... Mechmet* is as follows. Being a Servant to the Prince Sultan *Achmet,* and employed to cut Wood, and bring it to the Fire-Side, the Prince grew familiar with him, and would very often converfe with him concerning the News of the City.

One Day the Sultana *Valide,* coming into her Son's Apartment, to pay him her cuftomary Vifit, had among her Retinue a *Circaffian* Damfel, that very much pleafed the young Prince, who abruptly demanded her of his Mother She refufed to give her to him, in Conformity to a Cuftom eftablifhed among the *Turks,* which prohibits any junior Prince to propagate his Line. Prince *Achmet* waited the Opportunity of the Vifit, which his Brother, Sultan *Muftapha,* paid him from Time to Time, in order to beg the Girl of him. The Sultan's Refufal put him in a Rage · He fnatched up a Knife, and offered to ftab him · But the Grand Signior avoiding the Thruft, and willing

H 2

to

to ufe Moderation towards his Brother, perfuaded the Sultana *Valide*, who was his Mother alfo, to marry the *Circaffian* out of the Seraglio. This was foon done, and fhe was beftowed upon the Son of a Phyfician of the Court. Prince *Achmet*, having immediately heard this News from *Mechmet*, his Wood cutter, he commanded him to go in his Name to the Bridegroom, and tell him, that if it was his Fortune ever to come to the Empire, and he did not find his *Circaffian* a Virgin, he would exterminate him and all his Family. Such a Compliment as this very much frightened the young married Man, and made him become rather the Guardian Eunuch, than the Hufband of his Wife.

A little Time after, Sultan *Muftapha* was depofed, and Prince *Achmet* raifed to the Throne. His firft Thought then was, to make the Confident of his Amour, *Baltadzi Mechmet*, Mafter of the Horfe, and to order him to marry the *Circaffian*, upon the Condition he fhould never touch her. *Mechmet* obeyed, and the nuptial Prize was referved for the Grand Signior. The *Circaffian* became his Miftrefs, but out of the Seraglio; becaufe fhe had been already married to a *Turk*, though the Marriage was never confummated.

The Mafter of the Horfe, in the mean time, rofe in Dignity. He was made Vifir, but his Genius being too narrow, and infufficient to appear at the Head of Affairs, he had the Government of *Aleppo*, which is very lucrative, given him. After the Depofition of *Kouprouli*, the Grand Signior, having no Inclination to make the Campaign himfelf, and being unwilling to truft the Office of Grand Vifir to a Man of Abilities, the Power of that Minifter being then become arbitrary, he chofe for the intended Expedition

dition *Baltadzi Mechmet* Bashaw, as a Man incapable, for Want both of Genius and Courage, to confpire in the least Degree against his Master.

However, as he knew his Imperfections, he give him *Ofman* Aga, Receiver-General of the Customs, to be his Kihaia, that he might assist him with his Counsels, both in Affairs of State, and in War. This is a very important Employment in the Hand of a Man who knows how to make the most of it, and to become necessary to the Visir, a Secret which *Ofman* was not unacquainted with.

Mr. *de Voltaire's* Text.
Amsterdam Edition, p 318, &c. *English* Translation, p. 196, 198.

The Han of Crim-Tartary, *whom we call the Kam, had Orders to be in Readiness with forty thousand* Tartars —*This Kam, gained by the Prefents and Intrigues of the King of* Sweden, *got Leave at first that the General Rendezvous of the Troops might be at* Bender, *under the Eyes of* Charles XII, *to let him fee the better, that it was for his Sake that the War was undertaken.*

R E M A R K.

THE Han of the *Tartars* was fent for to *Conftantinople* before the Proclamation of the War. At his first Audience he received Marks of the Grand Signior's Favour ; a fable Robe, a Quiver, a Sabre, and two hundred Purfes of Silver, for the Service of the Campaign. After that publick Prayers were made, the Horfe-Tails were fet up before the Seraglio, and War was proclaimed.

A little before this Proclamation, an Envoy Extraordinary from *Auguftus,* King of *Poland,* arrived at *Conftantinople.* His Name was M. *de Bakowski* ;

Bakowski; and his Bufinefs to bring Advice, according to Cuftom, of a folemn Embaffy from the King and Republick. Count *Chomentowski*, Palatine of *Mazovia*, was charged with that Commiffion ; and *Bakowski* informed the *Porte*, that he was now preparing to fet out from *Warfaw*. The Envoy was received with all the cuftomary Honours, had his Audiences, both of the Grand Vifir and the Sultan. Yet, fo did *Poniatowski* manage Matters, that, notwithftanding his publick Reception, this very Minifter was afterwards fent under a ftrong Guard to the King of *Sweden*, as a Prifoner, whom his Majefty might difpofe of as he thought proper.

This Procedure was not perfectly regular : But the King's Will was obeyed ; and the Credit of *Poniatowski* appeared on this Occafion in its full Extent.

There was not, in this Meeting, any Difpute about the Ceremonial ; nor was it made a Queftion whether the Troops fhould affemble at *Bender* or at *Belgrade*; but they were to march on the Side of the *Danube*, over which Orders were given to the Prince of *Moldavia* to build a Bridge, in a Place called *Gachtzchia*.

The Czar had fecret Intrigues with the Princes of *Moldavia* and *Walachia*, the firft of whom went early to join him. The other contented himfelf with fending his Son-in-Law, and five thoufand Men. They both concluded, beforehand, that the *Mufcovites* would be victorious.

The Czar had alfo fent into *Albania* one *Sawa*, a *Ragufan*, formerly Interpreter to the *Englifh*, to raife an Infurrection among the *Greeks* againft the Grand Signior. He was himfelf fo confident of his approaching Victories, that he declared he would be buried at *Conftantinople*; which perhaps

he

he might have been, without conquering that City, if the Grand Vifir had followed the Counfels of Count *Poniatowski*.

M *de Voltaire*'s Text.

Amflerdam Edition, p. 321—338. *Englifh* Tranflation, p. 198—209.

The new Vifir, Baltagi Mehemet, *not being under the fame Engagements, (as the Kam of the* Tartars) *would not flatter a foreign Prince fo far. He recalled the Order, and this great Army was drawn together at* Adrianople.——*As foon as the Grand Vifir received the News, that* Peter Alexiowitz *was marching into* Moldavia,—*he proceeded to pafs the* Danube *upon a Bridge of Boats near* Saccia,——*and formed an entrenched Camp.*——*The Czar ---found himfelf without Provifions, between the* Pruth *and an hundred thoufand* Turks,---*In this Extremity he faid publickly,* ' *I am at leaft in* ' *as bad a Situation as my Brother* Charles *was at* ' Pultowa.' --*They agreed that it was necefjary to fue for Peace to the* Turks,---*and the Treaty was concluded and figned the* 21ft *of* July, **1711.** --*The King of* Sweden, *enraged, went directly to the Grand Vifir's Tent, and reproached him for this Treaty.---* ' *Was it not in your Power, faid he, to carry the* ' *Czar Prifoner to* Conftantinople?---' *And who* ' *fhould govern his Empire in his Abfence?'* anfwered *the* Turk. ' *It is not fit that all Kings* ' *fhould be out of their Kingdoms.'* ---Charles, *full of Indignation,---threw himfelf down upon a Sopha, ftretched out his Leg, and entangling his Spur in the* Turk's *Robe, tore it ; then rofe up immediately, and returned to* Bender *full of Defpair.* Poniatowski *continued fome Time longer with the Grand Vifir;--but, it being* Prayer-Time,--- *the* Turk *went to wafh himfelf, and attend his Devotion.*

R E-

REMARK.

IT is neceſſary to know, that the *Turks*, when they make War in *Europe*, always halt for ſix Weeks at *Adrianople*, either to give Time for the *Aſian* Troops to come up, or to put their Horſes to Graſs, which they pretend enables them the better to undergo Fatigue.

The Grand Viſir, who had no more Courage at a Diſtance than near an Enemy, ſtopped there, according to Cuſtom, notwithſtanding the News he received of the Enemy's having entered *Moldavia*: And he retarded his March as much as poſſible, to avoid coming to an Engagement with the *Muſcovites*; believing, according to the Hoſpodar of *Moldavia*'s Relation, that their Troops amounted to an hundred and fifty thouſand Men, and their Artillery to ſix hundred Pieces of Cannon.

Count *Poniatowſki*, manifeſtly perceiving the Falſhood of this Report, repreſented to the Grand Viſir, and his Council, that theſe Rumours were ſpread only to intimidate them, and to ſlacken their March, that the Enemy might have Time to ſeize the Bridge that had been built upon the *Danube*, and then to beſiege *Bender*.

The Solidity and Vivacity of his continual Remonſtrances, joined to the Suſpicions they began to entertain of the Hoſpodar of *Moldavia*'s Intelligence with the Czar, made the *Turks* reſolve to march on, which they did with ſo much Expedition, that at five Days End the Grand Signior's Armies were on the other Side of the Bridge upon the *Danube*. There the Grand Viſir, having heard of the Prince of *Moldavia*'s Defection, and found what was the Tendency of his Relations concerning the Greatneſs of the *Muſcovite* Army, returned Thanks to Count *Poniatowſki*

atowski for his good Advice, promised him
Mountains of Gold from the Grand Signior, and
from himself a Present which the *Turks* set a very
high rate by, no lefs than the Choice of two
pretty Girls from among fixty of the handfomeft
Slaves in his Seraglio, to refrefh himfelf with at
his Return to *Conftantinople* from the Fatigues of
the Campaigns

The Grand Vifir ftaid there ten Days, to give
his Army Repofe, and land the heavy Artillery,
which had come by Sea. He then fent for the
Han of the *Tartars*, to deliberate with him upon
the Operations of the War, and intreated Count
Poniatowski to take a Turn to *Bender*, and invite
the King of *Sweden* to their grand Council.

In the mean time, the Czar made himfelf
Mafter of *Moldavia*. He detached General *Renne*
with fome Regiments of Dragoons, and the *Wa-
lachians*, to feize *Brahilow*, a Place fituated upon
the *Danube*, above that where the *Turkifh* Army
was encamped. His Defign, in Appearance,
was to build a Bridge there, that he might with
more Facility penetrate forwards into the Country, and execute his vaft Projects

Count *Poniatowski* found the King of *Sweden*,
at *Bender*, fully refolved to repair immediately to
the *Turkifh* Camp. His Majefty, however, before his Departure, fent for his great Chancellor
Mullern, and Privy Councillor *Fief*, to ask them,
contrary to his ufual Cuftom, their Advice concerning what he intended. Thefe two Gentlemen,
tho' otherwife Perfons of great Probity, whether
they were piqued againft Count *Poniatowski*,
becaufe he had not been before-hand with them,
or whether thro' a particular Policy, referved only
for Minifters; or, laftly, whether it was through
a fad Fatality, reprefented to the King, that it
was not confiftent with his Majefty to be prefent

I   among

among such a haughty and contemptuous Nation, who had so much Regard for external Magnificence, without an Equipage suitable to his royal Dignity ; nor to serve, as a simple Voluntier, in a foreign Army. These Representations, and a thousand other Reasons, gave rise to some Deliberation, and made the King at last alter his Resolution.

Count *Poniatowski* was dispatched, with ill-digested Excuses, and even with an Order to persuade the Grand Visir to come to *Bender*, in order to concert there, with the King, a general Plan for a lasting War. The Count was extremely mortified at this, as well as at another unlucky Affair that arose afterwards from the same Source. It was, his not having been informed of a Letter which the Grand Signior had writ to the King, upon sending to *Bender* the Envoy of King *Augustus*; wherein his Highness promises his Majesty, that he will ever be his faithful Ally ; and that, if Heaven blessed his Arms, he would never make Peace with the Czar, except the Interest of the King were equally comprised in it with his own *Poniatowski* might have made an advantageous Use of such a Letter as this with the Grand Visir, when the Affair of *Pruth* was upon the Carpet.

At his Return to the *Turkish* Camp, he said all that he could think of to excuse his Master for not coming. But the the Grand Visir, turning towards the Han told him, that ' this was such an Answer as he expected, and that this haughty *Pagan* would never do them so much Honour.'

From that Moment, Count *Poniatowski* remarked in the Visir a great deal of Coldness towards his Person However, as this *Turkish* Minister had always found his Account in *Ponia-*
towski's

towski's Advice, he continued to make use of that, and had him still called to Council upon the least Intelligence of the Enemy's Motions. The Count, as he perceived the *Muscovites* were advancing, was of the Opinion to go and meet them. His Advice was followed, and, after a March of five Days, the *Turkish* Army arrived at the Banks of *Pruth*, over which it was necessary to erect Bridges.

Scarce had they encamped, when between seven and eight Thousand *Muscovite* Cavalry, under the Command of General *Ogilvi*, appeared, towards Evening, on the other Side of the River, and pitched a much more extensive Camp than was needful for such a Detachment.

The Grand Visir, who had never seen an Army, and was by Nature a great Poltroon, imagined that he should be inevitably lost, if the Enemies came to attack him. Count *Pontatowski*, judging by what they had done that they were only come to reconnoitre the *Ottoman* Army, and that their sole Aim, as well in the Extent of their Camp as in their great Fire, was to impose upon the *Turks* and make them believe that the whole *Muscovite* Army was arrived; concluded that they would retire in the Night, and did all in his Power to encourage the Visir, and persuade him to get the Bridges made with all Expedition.

What *Pontatowski* had foreseen, came to pass The Enemies Camp disappeared at Break of Day This animated the *Tartars* and the *Turkish* Van-Guard to swim the River, and follow *Ogilvi* They came up with him, and took some of his Men Prisoners.

The Visir resolved to lay the Bridges; and so much Expedition was used, that, in twenty four

Hours

Hours Time, two of them were finished. Over these the Army began to pass at Break of Day, and was all on the other Side about ten o'Clock in the Morning. The Men discovered a great Ardor for engaging the Enemy. But the Vifir, as there was now no River between them, obstinately infisted upon not advancing, and ordered Tents to be pitch'd.

Count *Poniatowski*, on this Occasion, had need of all his Eloquence to urge on the March, especially as he underftood, by the Relations of the Scouts who had followed *Ogilvi*, and by the *Muscovite* Prifoners, that the Czar now thought of nothing but retreating. But, as he could not overcome the Wilfulnefs of the Vifir, he told him, that all the Reports that had been brought him were falfe, that thofe who had overtook *Ogilvi's* Detachment, and gave out that they had defeated the Enemy's whole Army, impofed on him, and that, if he would let him have five or fix trufty Perfons, to go with him and reconnoitre their Camp, he would give him an exact Account of their Situation, and inform him what was neceffary to be done.

The Vifir, to get rid of his Importunities, granted his Requeft, and away *Poniatowski* rode full fpeed. He returned immediately, and redoubled his Sollicitations, offered to anfwer for the Event with his Head, and ventured to promife that he would put the Czar's Perfon into the Vifir's Hands, if he would but march againft the Enemies, who were already at their Wits End, and had been oblig'd to draw up their whole Army in a Square, to defend themfelves againft the *Tartars* of the *Turkifh* Van-Guard. But that if he neglected that fingle Day, the Enemy, who had but a League from the Place where they were to the Entrance of a Foreft, would take Advan-

tage

tage of the Night ; that by this Means the Glory
of a Victory would flip out of his Hands , that it
was neceffary therefore to haften the March, before the *Mufcovites* could reach the Foreft ; that
they had not a Moment left for Deliberation, but
that he muft take his Refolution that Inftant.
The five *Turks*, who had followed *Pomatowski*,
and whom he had inftructed to make Remarks
upon the Situation of the Enemies, could not a-
void giving in a juft Report

The General of the *Turkifh* Army, who were
prefent at thefe Relations, formed from them an
advantageous Idea, and great Hopes of Victory ;
and, joining all their Perfuafions to thofe of Count
Pomatowfki, they were fo powerful, that at laft
the Grand Vifir was obliged to march , but all the
Way threatening *Pomatowski*, that his Head
fhould pay for it, if they did not fucceed.

As foon as the Troops were upon the March,
the Count put himfelf at their Head, with the
Aga of the Janiffaries, and the Vifir's Kihaia his
particular Friend   The Grand Vifir brought up
the Rear, and they all advanced with great Expedition.

The *Mufcovites*, upon Advice that the *Turks*
were building of Bridges, had ordered three Hundred Foot Soldiers to fail down the *Pruth* in
fmall Boats, and endeavour to break them down,
or to burn them.   All the Men of this whole Detachment were taken Prifoners, and brought before
the Grand Vifir ; who made the Army halt, to
divert himfelf with cutting off the Heads of thefe
poor Wretches.   Count *Pomatowski*, feeing the
Army ftop, rode to know the Reafon of it.   He
furprifed to behold the barbarous and ill timed
Amufement of the Vifir , and fo effectually reprefented the Enormity of this Proceeding, that
he

he faved the Lives of an Hundred and Fifty of thefe miferable Prifoners, and got the March to be continued.

When they came in fight of the Enemies, and had advanced within Musket-Shot of them, they halted a fhort Space, to difpofe the Attack on the Side they thought proper. But the Janiffaries, full of Ardor and good Refolution, kept ftill advancing, without attending to the Orders; and, fetting up a frightful Outcry of *Allah! Allah!* many Times repeated, to invoke the Affiftance of God according to their Cuftom, they fell upon the Enemies Sabre in Hand, and would certainly have forced them in this firft and vigorous Attack, had it not been for the *Chevaux de Frife*, which the *Mufcovites* had thrown before them.

A general Difcharge at the fame Time, almoft in their Faces, not only allayed the Ardor of the Janiffaries, but put them in Confufion, and obliged them to a precipitate Retreat. The Kihaia and the Aga of the Janiffaries put to the Sword thofe that they met flying, and endeavoured to make the Troops ftop, and recover their Order. The moft brave among them renewed their Cries, and gave a fecond Attack · But this was not fo vigorous as the firft, and the *Turks* faw themfelves obliged to retire once more. The Kihaia then faid to Count *Poniatowski*, ' My Friend, we run the Risk of being beat, and we fhall be fo infallibly.' The Count, having obferved that the Enemies made no Advantage of the Diforder caufed among the *Turks*, but kept ftill firm in their Squaie, gave in Anfwer, that, ' far from being beat, he congratulated him before-hand upon a certain Victory, efpecially if they did but advance with a little more Order than they had hitherto done, becaufe the
Enemy

Enemy was only on the Defenfive.' It begun already to grow dusk, when the *Turks* gave another Attack with the fame Cries, and in the fame Manner; but this too was ineffectual.

The two *Turkifh* Generals, the Kihaia and the Aga of the Janiffaries, uneafy at the fmall Succefs of their Attacks, were pacified by the Reprefentations of Count *Poniatowski*, with whom they held a petty Council to confult what they muft do. As the Count had continually, ever fince they fet out from *Conftantinople*, inculcated to them the Manner they ought to attack in, and how to form the Order of Battle, he thought they would have conformed to his Advice. But the Kihaia told him, that if they had the Misfortune to be beat when they followed a new Way of Fighting, the Fault would lie upon them; and that in fpite of any Excufe they could make, they fhould both lofe their Heads; he, the Kihaia, for having followed that Method, and *Poniatowski*, for having advifed it. But, added he, ' if we are beat in our ufual Difpofition, with which we have conquered fo many Countries, then Providence alone will be accountable for the Event.'

Count *Poniatowski* then gave his Opinion, that they fhould enclofe the Fnemies with a Ditch, to be worked upon all the Night, and wait the Arrival of their Artillery, in order to make ufe of it at Break of Day, affuring him, that the Cannon alone, of which they had five hundred Pieces, would be fufficient to deftroy the whole *Mufcovite* Army. The Kihaia promifed to do fo, and immediately gave his Orders thereupon, leaving the Janiffaries in the fame Place where they had begun to attack.

The *Turks* afcribe much to Providence, and ftrongly believe in Predeftination. The Anfwer which

one

one of them gave to Count *Poniatowski*, will give a general Idea of their Sentiments thereupon.

A Gentleman-like Sort of a Man, belonging to the Grand Vifir's Court, being extremely well mounted, did nothing but make Excursions during the whole March from *Constantinople* He every Day tried several Horses His Skill in managing his Horse, making Use of his Lance, and wheeling about, was admired by every Body, even by Count *Poniatowski* himself, who asked the Kihaia one Day, What Man that was ? He answered, that the Man, besides his great Address, had an extraordinary Share of Courage ; and that, having often been a hunting upon the Frontiers of *Perfia*, he with his own Hand had killed four Lions.

On the Day of the Attack, this *Turk* followed the Kihaia in the Action: But he contradicted the good Opinion they had conceived of him, and shewed the utmost Timidity, pulling the Kihaia continually by the Sleeve, and in plain Terms persuading him to retire. *Poniatowski* remarked his Uneasiness, and, to make the *Turkish* General a little merry, bid him send his *Hector* to hunt Lions, since he could fight nothing but Beasts.

The next Day, Count *Poniatowski* dining with the Kihaia, and the Conversation falling upon the preceding Day's Action, when much was introduced concerning Destiny, *Poniatowski* made some Remarks upon the false Bravery of the famous Lion-hunter, who was also at Table. But the latter, without discomposing himself in the least, gave this simple Answer: ' How do you know if I was not predestinated to fly Yesterday ? Another Time, perhaps, it will be my Turn to pursue.' The Laughers, however, were

not

not of my Gentleman's Side. But let us return to the *Muscovites*.

They were certainly in the most scurvy Situation that can be imagined: Surrounded on one Side by the *Turks*, and having the River before them on the other, the opposite Bank of which was guarded by fifteen thousand *Tartars*, *Turks*, and *Poles* of the Palatinate of *Kiovia*, who incommoded them extremely with Volleys of Musket Shot, that they had no Possibility of escaping.

The Night growing very dark, the Kihaia and Count *Poniatowski* waited again on the Grand Visir, and found him trembling, though he was out of Cannon's-reach. After a short Conversation, *Poniatowski* retired to repose himself in a small Barrack, which his People had pitched near the Grand Visir's Tent.

Some Hours after, hearing the Noise of Carts that were not greafed, he sent to know the Meaning of it. His Emissary brought him Word, that they were *Muscovite* Carts; but, that he could not well distinguish what they carried. At Break of Day he went to his Friend the Kihaia, and told him his Sentiments concerning these Carts. But was answered, that in all likelihood it was the Booty which the Janissaries, or some others of the Army, had made. He then asked him, if he would not mount his Horse, to see what was to be done. The Kihaia seemed to give his Consent with Pleasure, but told him, that they must first go and see the Grand Visir.

At that Instant, the Guard brought an Aid de Camp of General *Szeremetoff*'s, with a Letter to the Grand Visir, in which the *Russian* General, after having affectedly attributed, with much Exaggerations, the Cause of the War to the Czar's Enemies, proposed to come to a Treaty. The

K   Grand

Grand Vifir defiring to know Count *Poniatowski's*
Sentiments of the Matter, the Count replied
that there was no need to give an Anfwer in
hafte, nor to capitulate with People whom Neceffity had reduced to that Extremity, that they
muft all furrender Prifoners of War; and that
the Attack ought to begin, and the Artillery to
play   He then whifpered the Kihaia, and they
both went out of the Vifir's Tent, and mounted
their Horfes, to make the neceffary Difpofitions.
They examined the Situation of the Enemies,
without firing a Shot on one Side or the other.

The right Wing of the *Mufcovites* appeared to
be thinner of Men than the left; which exten-
ding over a Ground that was fomewhat marfhy,
was confequently lefs entrenched. *Poniatowski*
made the Kihaia obferve this, and obliged him
to order the Artillery to begin to play on all
Sides, while the Men got ready to make
feveral Attacks at once.   At that Moment Word
was brought the Kihaia, that the Vifir commanded him to forbear firing, for that the Enemies defired to capitulate, and were juft on the
Point of fending their Ambaffadors.   The Kihaia not daring, as he faid, to contradict this,
gave Orders, that they fhould ceafe firing, and
rode up to the *Mufcovite* Entrenchments, to fee
what was doing there.

Count *Poniatowski* made him again remark
the Poffibility there was of attacking them very
eafily, and breaking them at the firft Shock; their
Entrenchments being but very fhallow, and full
of Water up to their Knees.   They all appeared
rather Dead than Alive, and the Want of Victuals
compleatly made their Situation the worft and
moft grievous that could be

When they went round the Intrenchments,
three *Mufcovite* Officers came out to them, one
of

of whom had known Count *Poniatowski* particularly at *Conſtantinople* The Count had recommended him to the King of *Sweden*, as a Man fit for his Service. He had even been at *Bender*, where the King made him a preſent of three hundred Ducats, in recompence for his Good-will, and gave him a Paſſport to go into *Poland*. This Officer addreſſed himſelf to the Count, and told him, that the Czar his Maſter had ſent him, with the other Officer, to ſue for Peace ; and that the King of *Sweden* might obtain all that he wiſhed for, provided that he, Count *Poniatow*, would intereſt himſelf in the Affair. *Poniatow*, who thought of nothing but taking the Czar and all his Army Priſoners, reproached the Officer for his Infidelity and Impoſture, in that he had made no other Uſe of his Recommendation to the King of *Sweden*, than juſt to go to his Enemies : Then went on, without hearing him any further, and, with the Kihaia, returned to the Grand Viſir's Tent.

That Miniſter, ſwelled with Pride like a Toad, asked Count *Poniatowski* ' if he did not admire at the many great Things he had done, before he had been yet a Year Viſir'? After a very ſhort Compliment upon his good Succeſs, *Poniatowski* told him, that ' he was well pleaſed to ſee his Predictions accompliſhed , but, that it was now in his Power to get the Czar into his Hands, make all his Army Priſoners, and his whole Country tributary.' The Viſir then told him, that he deſired to have his Thoughts in Writing , and Count *Poniatowski*, by his Interpreter, had them minuted down in *Turkiſh*. They conſiſted but of two Points , ' 1ſt To make the Czar come before him, and ſend him immediately to the Grand Signior. 2dly. to make all his Army lay down their Arms, and ſurrender

K 2   Priſoners

Prisoners of War. What was to be done further would appear afterwards.' The Grand Visir had them read out aloud, and put them in his Pocket, without saying a Word to them.

Count *Poniatowski* had sent that Day to *Bender*, very early in the Morning, to inform the King of *Sweden* of all that passed. He went immediately out of the Visir's Tent, after the Conversation above, and was told, that the Czar's Plenipotentiaries were coming.

It had been agreed with the Count, that the Visir should not hear these Plenipotentiaries, nor should they be brought before him, but have their Audience in the Tent of *Hummer Effendi*, Secretary of State. This Tent was got ready for that Purpose, and immediately filled with People. But the Plenipotentiaries, instead of alighting there, rode directly to the Grand Visir's Tent, and were introduced by the *Capigi* Bashaw, who had conducted them thither.

As soon as they appeared, instead of meeting with a rough Reception, Stools were called for, in order for them to sit down. This began to put Count *Poniatowski* very much out of Humour. It was natural for them to set forth the Subject of their Mission. But the Grand Visir prevented them with a *Hos Geldy*, which is a very friendly Sort of Salutation, and bid them be seated. Then observing Count *Poniatowski*'s Interpreter standing on one Side, he called him, and bid him ask the Plenipotentiaries, ' What they came to do in the ' Grand Signior's Territories?' Adding, ' That ' they had desolated *Moldavia*, and that the Visir ' required Satisfaction, which was the Restitution ' of *Afoph*; that he wished to have *Taigamrock* ' and *Kamienny-Zaton* demolished ; and that he ' demanded their Artillery.'

The

The Plenipotentiaries, furprifed at all this Le-
nity, and a Reception that they had no Room to
expect, anfwered, ' That they had paid for what
' they had had in *Moldavia* ; that the Invafion of
' the *Tartars* into their Territories, the preceding
' Winter, had obliged them to feek Revenge ;
' that, to prefeive the Grand Signior's Fiiendfhip,
' the Czar would reftore *Afoph*, and rafe *Taigan-*
' *iork* ; but, that *Kamienny-Zaton* was neceffary
' to him, to cover him from the Incurfions of the
' *Tartars*.' And as they were afraid, they faid,
of forgetting fome of the Vifir's Demands, they
prayed them to let them be put in Writing For
which Purpofe the Vifir fent them into the Secre-
taiy's Tent.

As they went out, they asked who that Man
was that had ferved them for an Interpreter ? And
being informed, that he belonged to Count *Poni-*
atowski, they protefted againft him, and required
to have either the Interpreter of the *Porte*, who
was not there, or their own.

While they were in the Tent of the Secretary of
State, Count *Poniatowski*, perceiving that the
Carts in the Night had worked their Effect, took
Occafion to tell the Grand Vifir, ' That with all
the Advantages which God had vouchfafed him
over his Enemies, it was in his Power to require
of them, and to obtain, other Terms than had been
propofed , that he had the faireft Opportunity of
making all *Mufcovy* tributaiy, of fending the
Perfon of the Czar as a Prefent to the Grand Signior, of making all his Army Prifoners, of getting rid for-ever of fo dangerous an Enemy, of
ferving the King of *Sweden*, and of procuring, to
the Sultan his Mafter, fo great an Influence among
all Nations, that they would earneftly fue for his
Fiiendfhip : That, as it now was, he fhamefully
forgot the Glory of the Empire, and the Intereft
of

of his Master, that he had two hundred thousand
Witnesses of his Actions, and that, if there was
not found one among them all, who would bear
Witness to the Truth, he, *Poniatowski*, would
himself present Petition upon Petition to the
Grand Signior, to give him a thorough Insight
into all the Actions and Proceedings of the
Visir.'

The Minister, enraged in the highest Degree
at these sharp Reproaches, made in the Presence
of so many People, returned very abusive Language, and uttered severe Menaces against the
Count, who replied again in the same Strain, and
went out.

Half an Hour after, the *Muscovite* Plenipotentiaries returned into the Visir's Tent, and rene-
ed his Demands much in the same Ter , be-
, adding only, that they must vant their
Artillery to defend them in their March against
the Cossacks, who doubtless would insult them if
they saw them destitute of Arms

Then the Grand Visir, as if just waking from
a deep Sleep, told the Plenipotentiaries, that the
Works had a Guest among them, the King of *Sweden*, for whom he demanded a free Passage. To
which the Plenipotentiaries answered, that they
not only granted him a Passage, but that they
were ready to carry him upon their Arms. The
Visir, hearing this, uttered a loud Exclamation
upon the honest Intention of the Plenipotentiaries.

He insisted, however, upon having the Cannon, and Freedom for the *Cossacks*, that their
Country might become independent. M *Szaf-
irow*, one of the Plenipotentiaries, answered, in
order to satisfy him, that he might order the Pieces
that were in the Army to be told over, and that
the Czar would give him the same Number at *A-
zoph*, and of the same Bore, when that Fortress was
demo-

demolished; adding, that the Grand Visir was too just to demand *Asoph* in any other Situation, than what it was found in when the *Muscovites* took it; and that he might be sure, that the same Quantity of Pieces should be left there, as were found when it was surrendered by the *Turks.* The Grand Visir, charmed with this Answer, made another Exclamation, and declared that he could not in Justice demand any thing more. Mr. *Szàffirow* then prayed the Grand Visir, that he might depart with these Conditions, in order to get them ratified by his Master. This was granted him, while *Szeremetoff,* the second Plenipotentiary, remained in the *Turkish* Camp.

Count *Poniatowski,* quite in Despair, and sunk deep in Reflection, seeing that it was impossible to bring the Visir to more Reason, resolved to try another Method. For this Purpose he went to the Trench, threw a thousand Ducats among the Janissaries and Train of Artillery, who knew him very well, and animated them against the Grand Visir, telling them, that his own private Interest had induced him to make a shameful Peace, by which he deprived so many brave Men of many Millions, which they must have got by forcing the Enemy's Intrenchments, which they had still an Opportunity of doing, if they would but hearken to and follow him. But, whether they did not care to expose themselves any farther, or that they durst not attempt any thing without Orders, they took the Money, and lamented Count *Poniatowski,* without stirring.

The Count, grieved to the Heart, that this Stratagem had not succeeded, and full of confused Ideas, went to demand Audience of the Grand Visir, who having convoked his Divan, ordered the Count to be told, that ' he would be no
longer

longer fo paffive as he had been ; and that, if he forgot his Refpect in the leaft Particular, he expoſed himſelf to imminent Danger ' *Poniatowski* anſwered, ' that he had never had a Defign to affront the Grand Vifir ; that he reverenced his Dignity ; and that, if he had repreſented the Truth with a little too much Warmth, he would be more circumſpect for the future , but, that he had Things to ſay to him of the utmoſt Importance.' Upon which the Vifir, having ordered him in, and told him, ' that the Peace being once made, all his Repreſentations would be in vain ; and that he had nothing to do but to make himſelf eaſy, becauſe there ſhould not be a Syllable of the Conditions altered :' *Poniatowski* anſwered, ' That he did not come to infringe the Conditions, but to communicate to him ſome Reflections upon them.

He owned it was true, that he faw with Grief the Czar and his Army efcape ; but, that he ſhould be yet more forry, if the Grand Vifir ſhould fuffer himſelf to be deceived through his Credulity : That, having agreed upon the Conditions, it was to be prefumed that he had thought of the Means of getting them complied with. ' The Czar, faid he, being juſt upon the Point of having his Liberty, and faving his Army, who can affure the Vifir that *Afoph* ſhall be reſtored, the other Places demoliſhed, and all the Conditions executed.'

This ſhrewd Remark ſtruck the Grand Vifir and his Council dumb. *Poniatowski* was defired to retire for a Moment, that they might deliberate upon what he had faid. The Reſult of their Deliberations was, that Moment, that they would take Hoſtages. *Poniatowski* replied, that they were manifeſtly unacquainted with the *Mufcovite* Government , that the Czar would have very little Regard to his Subjects, even the principal of them,

them, to extricate himself from such a Difficulty as the present ; that they might see this,
and be satisfied that what he told them was
true, in the frequent Examples of Execu-
tions that he made of Hundreds of Men at a Time,
upon the slightest Accusations, and even without
examining, whether the Charge was true or false.

They then sent out the Count once more, to
consider of other Expedients ; and, having called
him in immediately after, they told him, that
England and *Holland* should be Guarantees of the
Treaty made with the Czar, as they had been to
the Peace of *Carlowitz* To which *Poniatowski*
replied, that they had certainly a wrong Idea of
the Treaty of *Carlowitz* ; that those two Powers,
in Friendship with the Emperor of *Germany*, seeing the War with the *Porte* become more and more
burthensome to him, had then offered their Mediation ; that the *Porte*, finding itself almost in
the same Situation, had accepted it : But, that
neither of these Powers were Guarantees of the
Treaty , that a Difference was to be made between
Mediation and Guarantee ; that the Cases were
very different ; that, not to mention that the two
Powers were not required, they neither would
nor could any way meddle in the present Affair,
because, considering the Distance of their Dominions, it never could be in their Power to
oblige the Czar to keep the Treaty.

The *Turkish* Council thought to satisfy *Poniatowski*, by telling him, that they would cause the Embassadors of *England* and *Holland* to come from
Constantinople, and oblige them to the Guarantee.
But it cost him no Trouble to shew them the Impertinence of this Thought, when he represented to them, that the Embassadors,
not being instructed nor authorised by their

L   Masters,

Mafters, would never dare to do it before they had an Anfwer fiom their Courts, and that, befides their being uncertain whether they would have fuch an Anfwer as the *Porte* might wifh for, the Thing would take up above fix Months Time: That while they were waiting for it, the Czar and all his Army would be far enough off, quite out of their Hands, and relieved from the Circumftances of being obliged to keep the ftipulated Conditions.

The Vifir and his Divan, having nothing more to fay in Reply, told Count *Poniatowski*, that his Perfuafions were to no Purpofe; that they fhould not break the Peace in Compliment to his Reafoning; that they would proceed the next Day to the Ratification, unlefs he could find other Expedients; and that, if he had none, he had better keep his Advice to himfelf, as it tended only to embarrafs them. *Poniatowski* anfwered, that, provided they were not too hafty in the Ratification, the Expedient fhould be found; which was that as the *Turks* had room to doubt, if the Conditions of the Treaty would be complied with by the Czar, they ought to give Time to the King of *Sweden* to make his Terms with the Czar alfo; and, when that was done, the *Turks* would become Guarantees for the King of *Sweden*, and the King of *Sweden* for them; and in cafe the Czar contravened the Treaty, the *Porte* and *Sweden* fhould take Arms together, and make one common Caufe to oblige the Enemy to fulfil his Engagements.

This Expedient feemed to hit their Tafte. They ordered the Count immediately to form a Project upon the Plan of it, and even for the Peace itfelf, againft the morrow. It was to no Purpofe for him to repeat to them, that he had neither

neither the neceſſary Inſtructions, nor the full Powers from the King his Maſter. His Reaſons were not regarded. Seeing the Stupidity and Obſtinacy of the Grand Viſir, he promiſed to work at them all Night, on Condition that they would ſuſpend the Ratification, and not let the Enemies get away. The Viſir gave him his Aſſurance, that they would do nothing without compriſing the King's Intereſt, and that they would ſend him Word as ſoon as *Schaffirow* returned, that he might have Time to come to Terms with him.

Poniatowski, being retired to his Tent to work at his Project, had his Eye upon *Schaffirow*'s Arrival, and the Aſſurances of the Grand Viſir, whom he had all the Reaſon in the World to diſtruſt. At Break of Day, having heard that *Schaffirow* was come, he repaired to the Viſir's Tent, and placed himſelf behind him ; and, when the *Turk* had the Pen juſt ready to ſign the Czar's Ratification preſented by *Schaffirow*, without having even read it, he ſtopped his Hand, and put him in mind of his Promiſe : But, inſtead of being heard, he had for anſwer only theſe Words of the Viſir : *Where you have made your Quarrel, you have nothing to do but to make your own Peace.*

After the Signature, the Viſir gave Orders to let the *Muſcovite* Army inſtantly march out, to furniſh them with neceſſary Proviſions, which they were quite deſtitute of ; and even to give them an Eſcorte of five thouſand *Turks*, to reconduct them to the Frontiers of *Poland*, that the *Tartars* might not haraſs them in their Way.

While theſe Things were tranſacting, the King of *Sweden* came Poſt from *Bender*, and, as he arrived on the oppoſite Side of the River,

over

over-againft the *Mufcovite* Army, and faw their
Motions, and that they were intermixed with the
Turks, without any Injury being done on either
Side, not knowing what had happened, and quite
impatient to be informed, inftead of going to look
for a Bridge three Leagues off, he fwam his Horfe
over the River, and rode quite thro' the *Mufcovite*
Camp, without having a Word faid to him. He
fent an Officer before to inform Count *Poniatowski*
of his Arrival, who carried the News to the Vifir,
and mounted his Horfe to go and meet him.
When he came up to his Majefty, he gave him a
fhort Account of the Situation of Affairs.

The Grand Vifir fent two Bafhaws to meet the
King, to invite him into his Camp, and offered
him his Tent. He came out on Horfeback alfo
himfelf, with all his Court, who ranged themfelves before the Tent, to receive his Majefty.
After Reverence paid in their Manner, he introduced him into his Tent; where the King, having alighted, placed himfelf upon a Sopha on the
right, the Han of the *Tartars* in the middle, and
the Vifir in a Corner on the left. This laft opened
the Scene with a *Hos geldy faffa geldy*, which fig
nifies, *you are welcome*; and at the fame Time
gave a Recital of his Victory, and made his own
Panegyrick, mentioning what a few Months he
had been Vifir, and what glorious Things he had
already atchieved. The King having afked him,
'If he was not refponfible to his Mafter for having neglected to make ufe of his Advantage?"
he anfwered, with a haughty Stupidity, 'That
he was the Vicar of the Empire; that his Mafter,
having entrufted him with his Army and his
Power, had made him abfolute in War and Peace;
that having thought proper to make a Peace fo advantageous and honourable, the Grand Signior
would intirely approve of it; and that nothing

in the World could make any Alteration in it.'
While they were talking, Coffee was brought in,
and the King drank one Dish He then told the
Vifir, 'That his Mafter would have more Reafon
to be fatisfied, if he had the Czar in his Hands;
and if the Vifir would give him but twenty thoufand Janiffaries, he would take upon him to deliver that Monarch up yet.' The *Turk* anfwered by
an *Eftaforla*, that is, *God forbid !* ' The good
God, added he, has divided the World, and
given a Part of it to every Prince, for him to
govern. And who fhall govern *Mufcovy*, if I
take away its Prince ?' He concluded with faying,
' that Peace being once made, it fhould fubfift.'

The King, having heard this ftupid Anfwer,
went briskly out, mounted his Horfe, and rode to
vifit the Entrenchment. Count *Poniatowski*
fhewed him, at his Defire, the Difpofitions of the
Attacks. After which the King ordered him to
remove his Tents immediately to the Camp of
the *Tartars*, refolving not to return any more
into that which the Vifir had offered him He
lay among the *Tartars* all Night, and the next
Morning paid a Vifit to their Han, with whom
he continued an Hour, endeavouring to animate
him againft the *Mufcovites*. But not having been
able to bring him to a Refolution, he went to
Breakfaft with Count *Poniatowski*, whom he commanded to ftay in the Camp till his final Orders
came, and then fet out on his Return to *Bender*.

The Czar, well victualled and efcorted, marched away very contented at his having come fo well
off. He left with the Vifir *Schaffirow* and *Szeremetoff*, as his Hoftages and Plenipotentiaries;
and fent Orders to the Governor of *Afoph* to furrender that Place, and demolifh the others The
Vifir thought proper to wait in his Camp till the
Execution of the Treaty.

Poniatowski, abandoned to his melancholy Reflections, communicated them to his moſt familiar
Friends , crying out, without Reſerve, againſt
the Viſir's Procedure. The Kihaia, who had
ſtill a thorough Friendſhip for him, perſuaded
him to be pacified, and offered him a hundred
Purſes of Silver to comfort him , telling him, that
he (the Kihaia) was nominated by the Grand Viſir
to go and carry the Tiding of Peace to the Sultan;
and that he would not fail to do him Juſtice, with
regard to the good Services that he had performed for the Empire.

Poniatowski refuſed his Offer with Indignation,
and told him, that he had beſt take care he made
a faithful Relation to the Grand Signior , for
that his Highneſs ſhould know the Truth ſooner
or later : That in reality, if he endeavoured to
ſpare the Grand Viſir, inſtead of the Recompence that he promiſed himſelf for his good News
(which Recompence is uſually one of the beſt Go-
vernments) he ſhould be puniſhed for his Falſe-
hood.

The Grand Viſir had taken the Precaution, that
no Man ſhould paſs the *Danube*, without firſt giving
him Advice of it. As Count*Poniatowski* had reſolved
to communicate to the Grand Signior, all the Circumſtances of the Battle, and the Treaty, and the
many Faults committed by the Viſir , he wrote
down an exact Relation of the Campaign, and
propoſed to a Janiſſary, whom he had in his Service, and whom he knew to be entirely devoted
to his Intereſt, the Office of going to *Conſtantinople* at all hazards, and preſenting theſe Memoirs to the Sultan. The Janiſſary changed his
uſual Dreſs; and, pretending an earneſt Deſire
to ſee his Wife, entered himſelf as Servant to his
Brother, who was the Kihaia's Page ; and by this
Means

Means got to *Conftantinople* in the Kihaia's Retinue.

The Count had not fufficient Time to put his Relation in *Turkifh*, and therefore addrefled it to the Sieur *Brv*, Chancellor of the *French* Embafly, for him to tranflate it This obliged the Janiflary to wait till the following *Friday*, when he prefented it to the Grand Signior : who, after having read it, to prevent any one's knowing from whence it came, ordered the Janiflary to be clapped up in a Tower, with a ftrict Injunction not to let him fpeak to any Perfon whatever.

Collating this Memoir afterwards with the Kihaia's Relation, and finding them very different from one another, he fent for that Officer, and examined him very much, both on the Affair of *Pruth*, and on all the Reft of the Campaign. He then enquired concerning Count *Poniatowski*, to whom the Kihaia did Juftice, and, confefled, that he had performed very great Services among them. But, when the Grand Signior asked him, what was become of the King of *Sweden*, and whether he did not come to the Camp ? the Kihaia anfwered, that he did ; but, that he was a very unpolifhed Prince ; that he indecently fet himfelf down on a Sopha with his Legs dirty ; and that, though he knew the Peace was concluded, he asked the Grand Vifir for twenty Thoufand Janiffaries, that he might go and take the Czar.

The Grand Signior, though informed of all, ftill diffembled his Knowledge. But, inftead of giving the Kihaia the Government of *Egypt*, which he expected, he made him his Mafter of the Horfe ; telling him, that this was only to detain him near his Perfon, that he might at cafe hear his Relations, which gave him a great deal of Pleafure His real Defign, however, was to wait the Return of his former Mafter of the Horfe,

and

and the Haffeki Aga, whom he had fent, a few Days before the Kihaia's Arrival, to get Information of the Succefs of the Campaign. But let us return to the *Turkifh* Army.

Count *Poniatowski* taking the Air one Day on Horfeback about the Camp, met the Haffeki Aga his intimate Friend ; and having learned the Occafion of his coming thither, he took the Opportunity of giving him at large a Detail of all that had paffed. They went on talking, without perceiving that they were juft over againft the Grand Vifir's Tent, who, fufpecting the Subject of their Converfation, inftead of difpatching back the Haffeki Aga, put him under an Arreft, with an Order that he fhould fpeak to nobody.

The King had promifed Count *Poniatowski* to recal him, after he had procured the Liberty of certain *Swedes*, who, having been Prifoners among the *Mufcovites*, had made their Efcape, and got to the *Turks*, in hopes of becoming free. As there were among them the Muficians of fome of the Regiments taken at *Pultawa*, the Grand Vifir had a great Defire to detain them : But, being perpetually follicited by Count *Poniatowski*, he was obliged at laft to deliver them all up.

All this while he was not recalled ; and he ran every Day a great Risk of his Life. The Grand Vifir, whether he had got any Information of the Memoir prefented by the Janiffary to the Grand Signior, or whether he was piqued at the Count's repeated Complaints and Declamations, had taken the Refolution to get him affaffinated. *Poniatowski* was informed of it by mere Providence. One Day an Aga, or Gentleman of the Court, who had all along been near the Count's Perfon, by an exprefs Order of the *Porte*, of which the Count was wholly ignorant, came to wait upon him more early than ufual, and defired

fired to speak with him alone. The Aga was a *Pole* by Birth, but a Renegade in Religion. Having saluted the Count with a Good-morrow in the *Polish* Language, he opened his Discourse with a Torrent of Tears, and told him, that, in acknowledgment for the Civilities and Liberalities he had heaped upon him, he came to inform him, that he would be assassinated, before the Day was over, by Order of the Court ; that he, with his Comrade, and the Guards that were about him, had received Orders to withdraw ; that twelve Men, pretending to be drunk, would come to poinard him in his Tent ; and that his only Way was to take Measures for getting off as soon as possible. Two Hours after the two Gentlemen, and the Officer who commanded his Guard, came to take their leaves of him ; telling him, that they had Orders from the Visir to retire. The Count regaled them liberally at parting ; but from that Time his Thoughts were wholly employed on the Fate he expected. He did not say a Word of the Matter however to his Domesticks ; but only ordered them to have Coffee, Tobacco, Perfumes, and Sweetmeats, all in readiness, because he expected some Visitants. In the mean Time he furnished himself with two Pocket-Pistols, recommended his Soul to God, and waited for the fatal Castrophe of the Tragedy.

About Noon precisely, just as he had been informed, he saw the pretended Drunkards coming directly up to his Tent. They were no sooner entered, but he received them with great Politeness. Then calling his Servants, with a counterfeit Gaiety, and ordering them to bring the Coffee, Tobacco, Sweetmeats, &c. he earnestly intreated the *Turks* to sit down, and obligingly forced them to drink some Coffee, smoke a Pipe

M   of

of Tobacco, and partake of what elfe was there. The *Turks*, aftonifhed without Doubt at fuch a Reception, from a Man they were going to murder, did nothing but look at one another, without uttering a fingle Word ; till all at once, the chief of them, he who in all Likelihood was to begin the Execution, ftarted up fuddenly, and faid to the reft, *Heydygidelim* ; which fignifies, *let us be gone*. As he went out, he turned towards Count *Poniatowski*, and faid to him, *Ne Kiafir fen*, which is as much as to fay, *Thou art an extraordinary Heathen*.

The Count, having efcaped fo great a Danger by a fingular Providence, received, fome Hours after, the King's Order for returning to *Bender* Well pleafed with this News, as any one may imagine, he went immediately to take his Leave of the Grand Vifir , and, after fome ftrained Compliments on both Sides, they being both glad to get rid of each other, the Count fet out the fan Day.

Some time after, the Vifir received Advice, that the Commander of *Afoph* would not reftore that Place , for which he gave this Reafon, that, though he paid the utmoft Regard to his Mafter's Orders, he could not but look upon thofe, which were figned in the *Turkifh* Camp, to be extorted from him , and therefore would not deliver up the Place till he received others

The Grand Vifir, in the utmoft Confternation at this Incident, difpatched to the Czar Couriers after Couriers, to demand frefh Orders to the Commander of *Afoph*, and the intire Execution of the Treaty. The Czar was already a long Way off, and his Anfwer did not come. The *Turkifh* Army, weary of being kept in Camp without Neceffity, complained loudly, and infifted upon returning. Every body was diffatisfied, and reproached

proached the Vifir for not having followed *Ponia-*
towski's Advice.

Driven thus to Defpair, the Vifir wrote to the
King of *Sweden,* and prayed him to fend the
Count back, for that his Majefty's Peace with the
Czar might yet take Place. But the King anfwered, that he had need of the Count near his
Perfon , and that the Opportunity having once
been neglected, he could not now hope for fuitable
Conditions. Whereupon the Vifir fent Orders
to *Conftantinople,* that the *Swedifh* Envoy *Funk,*
who remained in that Capital, fhould be brought
to him with all Expedition.

When *Funk* was arrived, the Vifir told him,
that his Bufinefs was to make his King's Peace
with the *Mufcovite* Plenipotentiaries The *Swede,*
aftonifhed at fuch a Propofition, anfwered, that
he could not enter into any Negociation without
his Mafter's Orders, and the neceffary Inftructions; but that, if the Vifir defired it, he would
go and endeavour to get them at *Bender.* The
Turkifh Minifter would not confent to this, and
ordered him only to write to the King, detaining
him there till an Anfwer fhould come.

Though the Vifir's Propofition was quite un-
feafonable and ridiculous, his Majefty neverthelefs
fent certain Inftructions to Mr. *Funk.* But the
Negociation was broke off at the firft Conference
which that Minifter had with *Schaffirow.*

The Vifir, enraged without Reafon, through
his Ignorance of Affairs, put *Funk* under an Arreft, and for the future followed only the Advice
of *Schaffirow,* who, as well as the Vifir, would
ftand in need of fome Expedient to bring himfelf off, in cafe the Treaty of *Pruth* was not executed.

In all Appearance, it was by the Advice of
this Councillor, that the Vifir, to dawb over the

Affront

Affront given to King *Auguſtus* in the Perſon of his Envoy *Bakowſki*, diſpatched two Orders to the Baſhaw of *Bender* ; the firſt, to bring off that Miniſter, and ſend him to the Camp , the ſecond, to ſeize Count *Poniatowſki*, and ſend him alſo to the Camp, with his Hands and Legs bound ; imagining, that the King of *Sweden*'s Inflexibility proceeded from *Poniatowſki*'s Advice.

The firſt Order having been executed with Eaſe, as the *Poliſh* Envoy had the Liberty of taking the Air round the Country upon h's Parole, the Baſhaw was in no haſte to proceed to the ſecond. On the contrary, either from his particular Friendſhip for Count *Poniatowſki*, or from ſome other Motive, he ſent his Son to him, to inform him, that it behoved him to keep on his Guard, to lodge near the King, and never to ſtir out alone ; and even, that if the Baſhaw ſhould at any Time require him to wait on him, he ſhould always refuſe ; and that he would, at a proper Time, be acquainted with the Reaſon of this Advertiſement, when the Storm was blown over.

In the mean time, the Viſir's Uneaſineſs augmented, in proportion as the Reſtitution of *Aſoph* was retarded. He was more afraid of the King of *Sweden* at *Bender*, than of his own Maſter at *Conſtantinople*. At laſt, after many Deliberations with his Privy-Councillor *Schaffirow*, he took the Reſolution of ſending to *Bender* three Baſhaws, with ten thouſand Spahi's, to ſerve the King for an Eſcorte, with Orders to oblige him to depart immediately ; and, if he refuſed, to bind him, put him in a Chariot, and carry him by Force out of the Grand Signior's Dominions ; of which Order the three Baſhaws were to give him notice.

The King of *Sweden*, informed of the Subject of this Meſſage, and what a menacing Compliment

ment he was to receive in the Vifir's Name, ordered out thirty Dragoons to make a Lane for
the Bafhaws to pafs thro', between his two Tents,
with their Bayonets at the End of their Muskets;
and in this Manner he admitted the *Turks* to an
Audience. Before they began to fpeak, he ordered his Interpreter to tell them, that he would
have them take care what they faid, and that
at the firft indecent Expreffion, that was contrary
to his Honour and his royal Dignity, he would
order his Guards to burn their Beards.

The Bafhaws, more than half dead at this Refolution, bowed themfelves to the very Ground,
and retired in the moft humble Manner, without explaining themfelves on the Subject of their
Arrival. They fent to tell the Vifir, that it was his
only Way to come himfelf, if he had a Mind to
perfuade the King; for as to them, they were utterly unable to threaten a Prince, before whom
every Man muft tremble. The ten thoufand
Spahi's continued at *Bender*, till the Grand Vifir
had repaffed the *Danube*.

This Minifter, tho' preffed by the Grand Signior to bring back the Troops, marched very
flowly, in expectation of receiving the Keys of
Afoph. The Grand Signior, tired out with thefe
Delays, examined the Kihaia, from Time to
Time, concerning the Affair of *Pruth*. One
Day the Converfation having turned upon the
King of *Sweden*, and the Kihaia continually calling that Prince a mad Man, becaufe he wanted to
take the Czar after the Conclufion of the Peace;
the Grand Signior was put out of all Patience,
to that Degree, that he caught up fome Weapon
which lay at Hand, and heartily belaboured the Ki-
haia; telling him, ' that it was he and the Grand
Vifir who were Madmen, and not the King of
Sweden.'

Sweden.' He then ordered him to be fhut up in the fame Tower with Count *Poniatowski*'s Janiffary.

Mean Time the Vifir diew neai *Conftantinople*, where the Keys of *Afoph* at laft arrived. The Grand Signior, tho' very much provoked at all his Faults, fent a Cafftan turned up with Sable, to be prefented him on the Road, as a Token of his Favour · But, at the fame Time, he gave the Aga of the Janiffaries Orders to arreft him, and offered the Vifiriate to that Commandei.

This was the fame *Juffuff* Bafhaw, of whom Mr. *de Voltaire* fpeaks in his fixth Book, p. 215, of the Tranflation. But, he was not a *Mufcovite* by Birth, but a *Georgian*, and had been bought by a Janiffary when a Child, for thirty Crowns. He was brought up among that Soldiery, and had been fo happy, as to rife to the Dignity of their Aga ; from which he was promoted to the Vifiriate, upon the Depofition of *Baltadzi*, who was fent to *Mitylene*, and foon after ftiangled.

In the fame Place our Author makes mention of *Chourlouly Ali* Bafhaw, who was Grand Vifir, when the King of *Sweden* arrived in *Turky*: But that *Chourlouly* was not now living, having been ftrangled fome Time after his Depofition, as we obferved in its Place. — But let us iefume the Thread of our Relation.

As foon as the King of *Sweden* heard of the Vifir *Baltadzi Mechmet*'s Depofition, he commanded Count *Poniatowski* to fet out immediately for *Conftantinople*, in order to excite the *Porte*, if poffible, to a frefh Declaiation of War againft the Czar, to obtain thofe Advantages which had been neglected in the Treaty of *Pruth.*

The Moment he arrived at *Conftantinople*, *Poniatowski* waited upon the new Vifir, who had been his Confident, and from whom he had con-
cealed

cealed none of his Correfpondences, and moſt fecret Intrigues in the Seraglio. This Viſir was, more
over, a Man who did not want Courage. But inſtead of receiving the Count's Compliment, upon
his Advancement to the Viſiriate, he looked angrily
upon him, and ſaid with great Warmth, ' Pagan,
I know all thy paſt Intrigues, and give thee
Notice, that the firſt Plot I ſhall find thee carrying on, I will order a Stone to be tied about
thy Neck, and have thee thrown into the Sea.'

A Reception ſo diſagreeable made a very ſtrong
Impreſſion upon Count *Poniatowski*'s Mind:
He mounted his Horſe, and returned very penſive
and ſorrowful to his Quarters. But, ſcarce had
he alighted, before a Haſſeki, an Officer of the
Seraglio, came to tell him, that his Maſter,
Boſtandʒi Baſhaw, wanted to ſee him, and that
he muſt wait upon him that Moment. *Poniatowski* told him, that he would not go, for that he was
indiſpoſed, and had ſomething to do at home.
The Haſſeki, aſtoniſhed at this Refuſal, went
away very uneaſy, and an Hour after there came
two others, with the ſame Demand. As he per-
ſiſted in refuſing theſe alſo, they told him, that
they had Orders to bring him either with or without his Conſent.

This Confeſſion, tho' very perplexing, made
Count *Poniatowski* take the Reſolution, in order
to prevent his being expoſed to the Eyes of the
Publick, and led along like a Criminal, to go
immediately whither he was required, and take
his Chance, tho he was not able to imagine
what would be the Reſult. A ſmall Boat waited
for him at *Tophana*, and he was conducted by the
two Haſſeki into the Garden of the Grand Signior's Seraglio, which he walked acroſs, and was
led into a Hall that ſtood ſeparate from the other
Buildings,

Buildings, and was richly adorned, with Orders to stay there and compose himself.

A few Moments after, the *Boſtandzi* Baſhaw arrived ; and, having ſaluted him very gracıouſly, told him, that the Grand Sıgnıor, being at the Window, when he went out from the Vıſir, had obſerved him to be very penſive. ' It appeared to him, added he, that thou haſt been made uneaſy ; he commands thee to tell him poſitively what is the Matter.' Upon this, Count *Poniatowſkı* related the whole Story, without Heſitation ; giving this for the Reaſon of his Refuſal to come into the Seraglio at the firſt Summons, that he was afraid of ſome Snares being laid for him by the Grand Vıſir, who ſeemed to be ſo much irritated againſt him.

Boſtandzi Baſhaw quitted him at hearing this, and very obligingly deſired him to wait without Uneaſineſs. While he was gone, Coffee, Sweet-meats, *&c.* were brought to the Count, and he was ſerved with the all Ceremony of Dıſtınction. The Baſhaw kept him in waiting two Hours ; and when he came again, congratulated him upon his having the Grand Sıgnıor his Maſter's Favour, who, having heard with Surpriſe the Cauſe of his Uneaſineſs, had ſent immediately for the Grand Vıſir ; and, after long Converſation, had told him, that if the leaſt diſagreeable Thing happened to Count *Poniatowſkı*, he ſhould anſwer for it with his Head ' The Grand Sıgnıor, continued the Baſhaw, has commanded me to tell thee farther, that thou ſhouldſt make thy Addreſſes to the Grand Vıſir, in whatever thou haſt to propoſe, and take particular Notice of his Anſwers, in order to communicate them to his High-neſs in a Manner that ſhall be preſcribed to thee.'

It

It may well be imagined that such an Incident as this, proceeding from a Providence so visible, rejoiced the Heart of Count *Poniatowski*. He went home thoroughly satisfied, and laboured, more than ever, as well to be revenged on the Visir, as to animate the Grand Signior to a second Declaration of War.

As there was always something wanting in the Execution of the Treaty of *Pruth*, Count *Poniatowski* made warm Remonstrances on that Head wherever he came. He took every Opportunity to wait on the Visir, who, inwardly enraged, but not daring to make any Attempt against his Person, answered his Questions and Objections either in an abrupt Manner, or by something very foreign from the Purpose.

The Grand Signior, after having permitted this Comedy for ten Months together, took the Resolution at last to declare War a second Time, and ordered the Visir to have the *Muscovite* Plenipotentaries carried to Prison, upon the Backs of Asses. But the Visir not to expose his Friend by such a shameful Cavalcade, let them ride on Horses. The Grand Signior made a Handle of this Disobedience to punish the Visir, and had him strangled the same Evening. Some Months before the Head of the *Kihaia*, whom he had imprisoned, had been taken off before the Seraglio; and *Humner Effendi*, the Secretary of State that we mentioned before, who was concerned in the Treaty of *Pruth*, had suffered the same Punishment.

Count *Poniatowski* was highly pleased at all this. But Affairs the mean while did not go on with the same Vigour as before the other War. The Grand Signior did not dispose of the Visiriate, but advanced *Soliman*, Bashaw of the *Divan*, to be Kaimacan, which Place he had before held after the Deposition of *Kouprouli*. This *Soliman*, who from the first had been a Friend of the *Muscovites*,

N   en-

endeavoured to mortify Count *Poniatowski* in e-
very Thing hecould . But theCount,protected by a
superior Power, little regarded the Kaimacan's
Procedings.

The Grand Signior, in the mean Time, made
slow Preparations for War. He determined to
make the Campaign himself, and for that Purpose, removed to *Adrianople*. He sent two
Hundred Purses to the King of *Sweden*, and gave
Orders for the assembling of fifty Thousand *Tartars*, and twenty Thousand *Turks*, under the
Command of *Ismael* Bashaw, Governor of *Bender*, to escorte that Prince, that he might return
into his own Dominions, put himself at the
Head of his Troops, and make, in conjunction
with the *Porte*, a vigorous War against the common Enemy.

Things were upon this Footing, and the King
of *Sweden* had resolved to set out, when new In-
cidents, which it behoves us to unravel, changed
the Face of Affairs.

Count *Poniatowski* continued still at *Constantinople* ; but it was only to wait for Money from
Bender, in order to pay the Debts that he had
contracted for the King.

Before we continue our Narrative, we are o-
bliged to take notice, that, in the sixth and se-
venth Books of the History,which we have in part
endeavoured to clear up, the Author, seemingly
for want of faithful Memoirs, has given the Publick many Circumstances, which in Fact vary extremely from the Truth. Something, indeed,
of what he relates, really happened ; but he does
not relate it in Order of Time. Every Reader
therefore may see here a more just, and more con-
nected Account of divers particular Events, and
their true Causes. We pass over in Silence
the Affair of *Bender*, and some other Inci-
dents,

dents, which all the World are very well acquainted with.

Mr. *de Voltaire*'s Text.
Amflerdam Edition, tom. II. p. 8. *Englifh* Tranflation, p 213

All the European *Merchants refufed to lend the
King any Money, becaufe he feemed out of a Condition of ever repaying it.Only one* Cooke, *an*Englifhman, *dared at laft to advance about forty Thoufand
Crowns , content to lofe them, if any Misfortune
happened to the King of* Sweden ; *and fure to make
his Fortune if that Prince lived   This Money was
brought to the King's little Camp juft at a Time when
they began to want every Thing, and to defpair of
any Refource.*

R E M A R K.

LA *Motraye* was, or pretended to be, a Mafter of
the *French* Language at *Conftantinople.* Count
Poniatowski fent him from *Conftantinople* to *Bender*, with Money that an *Englifhman*, Treafurer
of the Nation, advanced to the King.   Certain
Prefents from the King enabled this *Frenchman*
to travel ; as he did afterwards, and gave as an
Account of what he had feen.   But it was never
in his Power to know any great Matter of what
regarded the King of *Sweden*, and his Affairs in
Turkey.

M. *de Voltaire*'s Text.
Amflerdam Edition, tom. II. p. 12, 13.
Englifh Tranflation, 216.

Conftantinople, *after* Charles's *Retreat to* Ben-
der, *was become what* Rome *has often been, the
Center of all the Negociations of* Chriftendom.
Count Defalleurs, *the* French *Embaffador at the*
Porte, *was employed in fupporting the Interefts of*

N 2   Charles

Charles *and* Staniſlaus ; *the Emperor of* Germany'*s Miniſters in oppoſing them. The* Swediſh *and* Muſcovite *Factions claſhed.* —— England *and* Holland *appeared as Neuters; but were not ſo. The new Trade, which the Czar had opened at* Petersburg, *had an Influence on the Views of thoſe two trading Nations. The* Engliſh *and* Dutch *will be always for the Prince who follows their Traffick moſt ; and the Czar's was then a very advantageous Trade.*

R E M A R K.

TH E Author gives a juſt and true Idea of the Negociations of the Foreign Miniſters at *Conſtantinople.*

M. *de Voltaire's* Text.

Amſterdam Edition, tom. II p 24, *& ſeq. Engliſh* Tranſlation, p. 232.

In the mean Time General Flemming, *King* Auguſtus's *Miniſter and Favourite, maintained a private Correſpondence with the Kam of* Tartary, *and the Seraskier of* Bender. La Mare, *a* French *Gentleman, and Colonel in the* Saxon *Service, had made more than one Journey from* Bender *to* Dreſden; *and all theſe Journeys were ſuſpected.* — *At this very Time the King of* Sweden *cauſed a Courier, ſent from* Flemming *to the* Tartarian *Prince, to be ſeized upon the Frontiers of* Walachia. *The Letters were carried to him, and decyphered. There appeared plain Marks of a Correſpondence between the* Tartars *and the Court of* Dreſden.

R E M A R K.

AT the ſame Time that the King of *Sweden* prepared to depart, his People intercepted Letters from the Han of the *Tartars,* and *Iſmael* Baſhaw

Bashaw Seraskier of *Bender*, writ to the Great
General of the Crown of *Poland*, in which they
informed him, that he need not take Umbrage
at their Entrance into *Poland* with the King of
Sweden , for that, as soon as they saw him advanced five or six Leagues into the Country, they
should leave him and return ; and then the
Great General had nothing to do but to seize
him, and do with him what he thought proper.

On the other Side, Count *Steinbock*, after the
Battle of *Gradebush*, which he had won, made, by
the Instigation and Persuasion of Count *Flemming*,
an Armistice for some Months. This he did in
order to give his Master Time to make his Peace
with King *Augustus*, which *Flemming* assured him
would be done

They both of them even persuaded King *Stanislaus* to make a Tour to *Bender*, with Passports for
the Security of his Passage, in order to persuade
the King of *Sweden* to set his Hand to it. This
Armistice was known at the *Porte*, by the Care
of the *English* and *Dutch* Embassadors, sooner
than the King had Advice of it.

The Han of the *Tartars*, and the Seraskier of
Bender, having heard of the Interception of their
Letters, took care to have the Passage of the
Danube so guarded, that no Body might go over
from the King of *Sweden* ; who, they were a-
fraid, would inform the Grand Signior of their
Treason concerted against him. They urged his
Departure with all their Might ; and seeing that
all their Arguments were to no Purpose, they
dispatched to *Constantinople* one *Hussein Effendi*,
chief Secretary and Councillor of the Han, to
carry a Relation to the Grand Signior that was
quite false and fictitious.

In

In this Account, they accufed the King of *Sweden* with intending to make war againft the Grand Signior, out of a Pique at his having been forgot in the Treaty of *Pruth*. Adding, that he had made Peace with the *Mufcovites*, and King *Auguftus*, and that his perfifting not to fet out from *Bender*, was only to wait for the Arrival of his Troops, and thofe of his new Allies, in conceit with whom he was then to make War againft the *Porte*. The Emiffary, a Man full of Subtlety, joined fo many Circumflances to this Narrative, that the Grand Signior believed it. He fent however to the Embaffadors of *England* and *Holland*, to ask them, if they had heard any Thing of the King of *Sweden*'s Peace with his Enemies? Thefe Minifters confirmed the Fact, without diftinguifhing that this Peace was only an Armiftice; which the *Turks* always confound with a Treaty, becaufe they never make any Thing but temporary Truces with the Chriftians. It is reported, that the Grand Signior, upon this, fent Orders to the Han of the *Tartars*, and the Bafhaw of *Bender*, that they fhould bring the King of *Sweden* by Force, dead or alive, to *Adrianople*. Thefe Orders, however, were afterwards denied by his Highnefs.

The Han's Secretary, having acquitted himfelf of his Commiffion to the Grand Signior at *Adrianople*, made a Tour to *Conftantinople*. Count *Poniatowfki* having heard of his Arrival, and being familiar with him, went to wait upon him, to know if he had any News from *Bender*, whence the Count had heard nothing for fix Weeks before. He had indeed been much perplexed on that Account, becaufe he knew the King's Refolution to depart; and the Money did not come for Payment of the Debts. *Huffem* feemed in a Surprife to fee him at *Conftantinople*, and asked him

him what he did there, when the King of *Sweden* had been gone three Weeks from *Bender?* *Poniatowski*, who knew his Majesty's strict Honour, could not persuade himself that he had been thus left without any Notice of his Departure, and therefore told the Secretary, that he could not believe what he said.

However, as *Hussein* persisted in what he had advanced, the Count, knowing him to be extremely addicted to Liquor, had several Bottles of the strongest Wine brought in, and intreated his Friend to drink, to refresh himself after the Fatigue of his Journey. When the *Tartar* had got himself well filled with this Liquor, his Heart grew a little more open. He then told the Count, that, as he was his Friend, he must sincerely confess to him, that the King of *Sweden* had made his Peace with the Czar and King *Augustus*, in revenge for his having been forgot in the Treaty of *Pruth*; that, he was going to draw together his Troops, with those of his new Allies, to make war against the *Porte* But, that he would pay dear for his Folly; because he, the Secretary, had just now procured Orders to the Han his Master, and the Seraskier *Ismael*, to put the King and all his Retinue to the Sword: 'And thou, added he, wilt do well to go on board the first Christian Vessel, to make thy Escape from hence; for otherwise, thou wilt be treated in the same Manner.' He informed him also, that the Envoy of *Sweden* was already arrested at *Adrianople*, which indeed was true, and Count *Poniatowski* knew of it, but was utterly unacquainted with the Cause.

Such a surprizing Piece of News made the Count easily conceive, that these were the Inventions of the King's Enemies for his Destruction: And, without knowing any Thing of the Interception eeption of the Han and the Bafhaw of *Bender's* Letters, he concluded, that the Armiftice of General *Steinbock*, being interpreted to the Grand Signior to the King's Difadvantage, at the fame Time when his Majefty was doing all in his Power to ftir up the *Porte* to a War, was in all likelihood the Caufe of this, fo a fatal Refolution.

Having got rid of his drunken Companion, he waited upon one of his moft intimate Friends, the new Captain Bafhaw, of whom we fhall fpeak more at large a little farther, to know what News he had heard, and to communicate to him this which we have juft related.

The Captain Bafhaw owned, that there was fomething whifpered about very much to the King of *Sweden's* Difadvantage ; but, that he did not know any one Particular or Circumftance. He then directed the Count to get himfelf informed elfewhere, efpecially by the Boftandzi Bafhaw, and to bring him afterwards an Account of the whole. Boftandzi Bafhaw, another particular Friend of Count *Poniatowski*, had heard nothing at all of this Rumour ; but told him, that he would wait upon the Captain Bafhaw, to get Information what it arofe from.

Poniatowski made hafte back to the Captain Bafhaw, to inform him that the other would be with him immediately. Half an Hour after, the Boftandzi Bafhaw arrived. Thefe two great Officers of the Empire, convinced by the Reafonings of Count *Poniatowski*, their common Friend, of the Malignity of the King of *Sweden's* Enemies, and the Falfehoods they advanced in order to ruin that Prince, were perfuaded of the Injuftice that was done him, and of the Neceffity of opening the Grand Signior's Eyes.

They

They agreed, that it was neceſſary for Count *Pomatowſki* to write to all his Acquaintance in the Seraglio, and aſſure them, that the Ambaſſadors of the Chriſtian Powers threatened the *Porte* that all *Europe* would intereſt itſelf in the Affront given to the King of *Sweden*. The Captain Baſhaw was to get himſelf ordered to *Adrianople*, to the Grand Signior ; and Count *Pomatowſki* was to go with him, to endeavour to avert this Storm, if it was not already too late. Agreeably to this Reſolution, *Pomatowski* went to all the Ambaſſadors, and endeavoured to perſuade them to intereſt themſelves in the Outrages committed upon the King of *Sweden* : But, not one of them would ſtir in the Affair, except M. *Deſallew*, who wrote to the *Porte* in the Terms that had been conceited

Some Days after, the Captain Baſhaw received Orders to repair to *Adrianople* , and Count *Pomatowſki* ſet out with him. A ſhort Time before their Arrival, the Grand Signior had received, by Means of Colonel *Longuevelle de la Cerda*, a Petition from the *Swediſh* Envoy, who was under Reſtraint ; but it produced no Effect, and the Envoy was ſtill kept with ſomebody to watch him.

Count *Pomatowſki* paid his firſt Viſit to the Grand Viſir *Soliman* Baſhaw, who had been raiſed from Kaimacan to that Poſt He told him, that he was very much ſurpriſed to ſee their Envoy arreſted, and that all who belonged to the King of *Sweden* were treated as Enemies, without any Conviction, or Knowledge of the Cauſe He then waited upon the Maſter of the Horſe, and the *Rekiptar* Aga, Favourite of the Grand Signior's Stirrup, who were both his good Friends, to communicate to them his Thoughts. He ſaw himſelf alone at Liberty, while all the reſt of the

O   king

King of *Sweden*'s People were either arrested, or ill-used. He redoubled his Activity, and had such Success, that, upon his Persuasions, the Palatine of *Mazovia*, newly arrived as Ambassador from the King of *Poland*, was made a close Prisoner in his Palace, and the *Swedish* Envoy was released.

The vulgar Reports concerning the Affair of *Bender*, were advantageous to the King of *Sweden*. All the World agreed that he had had great Injustice done him, and People said so much in his Behalf, that the Grand Signior was alarmed at it. Hereupon he sent his Master of the Horse to Count *Poniatowski*, to tell him, that the . was not dead, that they were bringing . *Adrianople*, and that he would do well to . meet him, and persuade him to take the Blame on himself of what had befel him at *Bender* . Adding, that the Grand Signior would open his Treasures to him, and give him the Command of all his Troops, not only by way of Escorte to himself, but to make war against the *Muscovites*; and that he would punish the Han and the Bashaw of *Bender*. In effect, the first of these was deposed, and the other strangled, before the King of *Sweden* arrived at *Adrianople*.

In the mean time, the Visir *Soliman* was deposed, and *Ibrahim Motna*, Captain Bashaw, advanced in his Room He immediately sent for Count *Poniatowski* his Friend, and ordered him to assure the King of *Sweden*, as soon as he saw him, of his sincere Attachment to his Person; and that, when his Majesty came near *Adrianople*, he should be glad to see him, and to concert Measures together with him concerning a War with his Enemies, and his Majesty's Return to his Dominions, at the Head of a chosen Army.

Pon-

Poniatowski, having engaged the Vifir, that he fhould never admit the Palatine of *Mazovia* to an Audience, nor acknowledge him as the Ambaffador of *Poland*, fet out to go and meet the King, whom he found at *Karnabot*, twenty-four *German* Leagues from *Adrianople* His Majefty was fo much the more glad to fee him, as he had heard that he had been maffacred at *Conftantinople*; and entertained him a long while with an Account of what had happened at *Bender*. Though the Count well forefaw that the King of *Sweden* would never fubmit to a Meafure fo little conformable to his Character, as that of taking upon himfelf the Fault of the *Bender* Affair ; he however told him his Story, and informed him that the Han of the *Tartars* either was or foon would be depofed, that *Ifmael* Bafhaw was or would be ftrangled , and that his Majefty might have any other Sort of Satisfaction, if he would but accept of the Grand Signior's Propofitions. But, feeing that his Perfwafions had no Effect, he defired his Majefty to think of what was to be done.

The King promifed himfelf much from the Activity of the new Vifir, having heard him fpoke of as an extraordinary Man, and knowing that he had declared himfelf in his Love off Two Days after, Count *Poniatowski* fet out before his Majefty for *Adrianople*, where, at his Arrival, he found fome Variation from thofe pofitive Declarations, which the Grand Vifir had given him; the Palatine of *Mazovia* having been admitted to an Audience, during his Abfence , with all the cuftomary Ceremonies. He reproached the Vifir very bitterly, for not having kept his Word, after it had been given to his Mafter, exaggerating, with great Sharpnefs, the Irregularity of this Proceeding. The Vifir, furprifed at this warm Difcourfe, côurfe, found himfelf confufed, and did not know whether he had beft put himfelf in a Paffion, or diffemble his Anger; and in this manner they parted.

The *Turkifh* Minifter, having reflected on what had paffed, fent for Count *Pomatowfki*'s Interpreter, and told him, that his Mafter had forgot himfelf, that he had called him a Liar to his Face; and that if he, the Vifir, had not had a great Friendfhip for him, he fhould have been provoked to fome Violence. He then bid the Interpreter tell him, that he would do well to moderate his Vivacity, if he hoped to preferve his Friendfhip, and that he might wait upon him the next Morning.

This fecond Converfation was fpent in mutual Excufes. The Vifir alledged, that, in a Poft which obliged him to hear all the World, he could not difpenfe himfelf from giving Audience to the Palatine of *Mazovia*. But, that it would be proper to fend for the *French* Ambaffador to *Adrianople*, to confult with him what fhould be done. ' For, added he, we muft however convince the Grand Signior that the King of *Sweden* has ftill fome Friends among the Chriftian Princes, tho' the *Englifh* and the *Dutch* are at Work for the *Mufcovites*.'

All thefe ill-digefted Reafons gave Count *Pomatowfki* to underftand, that the Infinuations of the Minifters of thofe two maritime Powers had made an Impreffion upon the Grand Signior's Mind. He obferved, that the People no longer exaggerated fo ftrongly the Affront given to the King of *Sweden*, as they had before done.

Count *Pomatowfki*'s Excufes in behalf of the King, for his refufing to take on himfelf the Faults he had not committed, were not relifhed by the Sultan, and the Difpofition that this Empe-

ror

ror had fhewn for renewing the War with the *Mufcovites*, was very much abated. The Vifir, however, made Preparations for an Expedition, which he kept a Secret to himfelf. He had even fent Money into *Bofnia*, his native Country, to raife there thirty thoufand Men; and all this without the Grand Signior's Knowledge.

In the mean time, the new Han, *Kaptan Giery*, Brother of him that was depofed, arrived at Court; but he had feen his Brother in the Way, as he was going to his Place of Exile, and had been intreated by him to revenge his Caufe the firft Opportunity. Count *Poniatowski* went to vifit this Prince; and, after having congratulated him upon his Advancement, he had a long Confcience with him upon the prefent Situation of Affairs: But the Count found him extremely cold and full of Diffimulation, excufing himfelf that he could not freely enter into thefe Matters, as he had not feen the Grand Signior, and did not know his Intentions. *Poniatowski* even accompanied this firft Vifit with a confiderable Prefent; but all this was to no Purpofe. He perceived that Affairs would not run in the Channel he could wifh

Some Days after, the King of *Sweden* arrived, and was lodged at *Dimitarfh*, the Palace of a Vifir, an Hour's Journey from *Adrianople*. It had been reported, that he would be carried to *Salonica*, and there embarked, and fent to *Marfeilles*, but no fuch Refolution had been taken.

Two Days after his Majefty's Arrival, the Vifir told Count *Poniatowski*, that he would fee the King the next Day; and even gave Orders in the Count's Prefence, to have his Tents pitched at *Dimitarfh*. This being reported to the King, his Majefty prepared to give him Audience in his
Bed,

Bed, which he had kept ever-since his Departure from *Bender*.

Next Day the Visir, with the new Han, went into the Tents that had been erected for them. But, instead of waiting upon the King, they sent his Majesty Word, that they expected him to come to them. The King answered, that he was sick, as all the World knew; and that, if he was even in ever so good Health, it was their Duty to come to him, if they had any thing to say to him.

Upon this, the Visir sent for Count *Ponietowski*, and spoke to him in such a Manner as to let him understand, that he absolutely must persuade his Master to come without Hesitation; for that his Interests required it. But the Count having shewn him the Impossibility of ever persuading the King to a Thing so contrary to his Dignity, he sent for the *French* Ambassador, who arrived at *D......tash* two Days before to wait on the King.

M. *Desalleurs* saw fully the Visir's Impertinence, who was puffed up with his Authority: But it was his Opinion, that Necessity required Dissimulation, and he could have wished, that the King would have taken this Step. However, not finding his Majesty disposed to it, he endeavoured to excuse him as well as he could.

Thus the Visir, without doing any thing, and after having amused himself a whole Day in a fruitless Negotiation, departed for *Adrianople*. Having ordered Count *Ponietowski* to wait on him, he exaggerated the King's unreasonable Haughtiness, and insisted much upon his own Authority, by which he represented the Grand Signior. Adding, that he had, it was true, promised to go and see the King, but that he supposed his Majesty would have come to his Tent. After many Disputes and Reasons given on both Sides, he said at last, that, in spite of the King himself,

himself, he had still an Intention of reconducting him into his Dominions. He then convoked the Divan, to deliberate on that Affair

In this Council, *Selictar Ali* Bashaw, the Grand Sig ior's Favourite and Son-in-Law, who could make Affairs take what Turn he pleafed, juft as they fquared with his own private Intereft; and who was *Cubee Wsir*, that is, Bashaw of the Council, fpoke his Sentiment a little too freely. The Vifir, thinking his Authority wounded, treated him with injurious Expreffions, and threatened to have him fkinned alive, if he dared to oppofe his Will Selictar Bashaw, ready to buift with Indignation, held his Peace But, at going out of the Divan, he waited upon the Han of the *Tartars*, who was no Friend of the Vifir's, to concert with him the Means of Revenge

They formed their Plan well, and then went both to the Grand Signior, to tell him, that his Highnefs ran the Rifque of being depofed by the new Vifir, who diffipated his Treafures to gain the Good-will of the Janiffaries, that he levied Troops in *Bofnia* without his Highnefs's Knowledge, to have them at his own Command, and that while he was yet Vice-Admiral, he carried on a Correfpondence with the *Mufti*, in order to make himfelf Mafter of *Cyprus*, and enter into an Alliance with them againft the Grand Signior. They added other Accufations, fome of which were true

Mean Time the Vifir, fufpecting nothing, went on in his old Way He amufed himfelf every Day in fhooting at a Mark with the Janiffaries; and the moft dextrous were profufely rewarded, with Money that he drew out of the Treafuries.

One Morning, being in Converfation with *Poniatowski*, in whom he teftified a great deal of Confidence,

fidence, even so much as to communicate to him
his ambitious Designs, there came a Message for
him from the Grand Signior. He ordered Count
Poniatowski to stay till he came back ; and mounted his Horse, to ride to the Seraglio. An Hour
after came a Capitzi Bashaw full gallop, who en-
tering the Visir's Apartment with great Haste,
began to clap the Seal upon all the Doors and
Cabinets. When he perceived Count *Poniatowski*, whom he knew, he asked him, what he did
in that House ? The Count answered, that the
Visir had ordered him to stay. Upon which the
Capitzi told him, that the Visir had been torn to
Pieces, and thrown into the River ; that at his Entrance into the Seraglio, finding himself enclosed
betweeen two Doors, he defended himself most
desperately , and that he had killed two Men,
before they could seize him. This Officer then
advised Count *Poniatowski* to retire as soon as he
could , and the Count immediately set out
for *Demirtash*, to inform the King of this new
Revolution.

It is very certain, that this Visir had great
Designs in his Head ; and that if the Grand
Signior had not taken him off, he would have
been deposed himself.

It is proper to say a Word or two here of the
History of this *Ibraim*. He was of a fierce Tem-
per, but very brave. He had been above fifteen
Years a Highway-Robber, as he had himself related it to Count *Poniatowski*. He was a *Bosniac*
by Birth ; and as to Religion, he was neither
Turk nor Christian; yet more inclining to the
latter than the former. He had not one *Turk* in
his Court ; for he mortally hated them all, and
spoke of them with Contempt. Having reflected
upon his Manner of living, he quitted the Calling of a Robber, and came to *Constantinople*,
where

where he entered himself among the Watermen,
and got his Living by carrying of Passengers over
the *Bosphorus*

One Day the Grand Signior, in disguise, had a
Mind to cross over to *Scutari*, and accidentally entered himself alone in *Ibrahim*'s Boat. He observed
in the Waterman a very promising Physiognomy,
and asked who he was? *Ibrahim* gave the
History of his whole Life to the Grand Signior, without knowing him. Among other
Subjects, the Boatman spoke of Government, naval Affairs, and many other Things,
all with a great deal of Justice. His Discourse
very much pleased the Grand Signior, who, land-
ing without making himself known, left thirty
Ducats in the Place where he had sat ; and ordered *Ibrahim*, on such a Day, to come with his
Boat to a Door that he named to him.

Ibrahim did not forget the Appointment ; and
the Grand Signior being also there at the Time
fixed, again disguised, went into the Bark, to
cross the *Bosphorus*. The Boatman treated him with
more Reserve and Circumspection than he had
before done ; and when the Grand Signior asked
the Reason of this Shyness, he answered, ' Thou
must be something more than thou appearest to be :
Thy Generosity is an infallible Proof of it ' The
Grand Signior then owned to him, that he was his
Master ; but with an Injunction not to mention
it to any Body.

He then asked him if he was a Sailor ; and if
he had Courage enough to go into the open Sea
with his little Bark, and make a Voyage to
Candia? *Ibrahim* answered, that it was a dangerous Attempt , but, if there was an Occasion
for it, he would undertake it. Upon this the
Grand Signior gave him a Letter to the Bashaw
of the Place, bid him set out immediately, and

ordered

ordered him to bring the Bashaw over. *Ibrahim* obeyed, took Bread and Water for his Subsistence ; and, meeting with a favourable Wind, put off to Sea in the Grand Signior's Presence, and had the good Fortune to reach the Island. As soon as the Bashaw had received the Order, he went on board this little Boat, and came to *Constantinople*, where he landed at the Seraglio, in the Place that his Conductor shewed him. They were both brought before the Grand Signior, without being known to any Body. *Ibrahim* kept the Bashaw Company for some Days, without stirring out of the Seraglio.

The Grand Signior, having before concerted his Scheme, deposed the Visir that then was, and put in his Place the new Commander. *Ibrahim*, in Reward for his Expedition, was made Captain of one of the Grand Signior's Galleys.

As Vessels of this Sort are usually sent into the *Archipelago*, to raise the Capitation upon the Christians, *Ibrahim* was often employed in that Business Being once at *Rhodes*, whither the Han *Kaptan Giery* had been exiled, he learned that one *Molna*, his Enemy, was in the Han's Service. He demanded to have him, which the Han refusing, he broke open his Seraglio, committed Violences upon all his Women, took *Molna*, and had his Brains beat out with Clubs. The Han complained to no Purpose. He could not obtain the least Satisfaction.

Chourlouly Ali Bashaw, then Grand Visir, taking notice of *Ibrahim's* Favour with the Grand Signior, banished him to *Smyrna*, where he continued two Years in Oblivion But, either having heard of the Deposition of *Chourlouly*, or else been recalled by the Grand Signior, he came back to *Constantinople*, where he was made Vice-Admiral, then Admiral, and at last Grand Visir.

The

The Han *Kaptan Giery*, having been at the same Time advanced in the Room of his Brother *Dewlet Giery*, and remembring the ill Treatment at *Rhodes*, joined with the Selictar Bashaw to displace *Ibrahim*, in which they succeeded as above.

Let us now fee what the King of *Sweden* did at *Demirtash*, where he continued for some Time in Oblivion

The Selictar *Ali* Bashaw (the same whom the Author of the History * calls *Ali Cumourgi*) being made Kaimacan after the Deposition of *Ibrahim*, refused to have any Commerce with the *Swedes*. He ordered the Envoy *Funk* to be seized by the Guard, and carried to *Demirtash*, to keep the King Company He sent to Count *Poniatowski*, to tell him, that he too must go to his King. The Count alledged in Excuse, that his Business was at the *Porte* : But he was told, without Regard to his Reasons, that it behoved him to follow the Advice that was given him ; that they shewed him the more Regard, on account of the Services that he had rendered to the *Porte* , that they were unwilling to offer him the Affront and Shame of being carried thither by the Guard , but, that they advised him, in sincere Friendship, to submit to these Representations without Reply ; because that otherwise, the Kaimacan would make use of Force.

All the Negociations and Intrigues, that had been begun under the Sanction of *Ibrahim*, the Grand Signior's Coufin, were then put a Stop to, As this Prince died suddenly, he was thought to be poisoned ; and there was good Room to think that this Suspicion was well founded. In the midst of all the preceding Convulsions, and

---

* Page 265, 266, 267 of the Translation.

while

while *Ibrahim* lived, there always appeared some
good Intention towards King *Stanislaus*, and an Inclination to re-establish him in *Poland:* But upon
this last Change, he seemed to be treated as a Prisoner; and the King of *Sweden* was entirely abandon'd
at *Demirtash.* The Plague broke in there among
the *Swedes*, and many of them died of it. Befides, the Want of Necessaries was every where
felt. King *Stanislaus* was in a perplexing Situation. At last, he took the Resolution of leaving
the Country, as the Persuasion of the *Turks* · And
the King of *Sweden*, being in Pain for him, ordered Count *Poniatowski* to endeavour to join
him, to conduct him to the Dutchy of *Deux Ponts*,
and to get h m supported there.

Poniatowski, accordingly, came up with him
at *Jaffy* , accompanied him through *Transilvania*,
Hungary, *Austria*, and the whole Empire , and
happily conducted him to *Deux Ponts*, without
any sinister Accident. As he passed by *Vienna*,
Prince *Eugene* gave him one Lieutenant-Colonel
Weiss, to take care of his Safety on all Accounts.

Count *Poniatowski*, having rested only three
Days in *Deux Ponts*, returned into *Turkey*,
and found the King of *Sweden* at *Demotica*, whither his Majesty had removed from *Demirtash*.
There, being chagrined at seeing himself thus forgot, as if he had not been among the Living, and
not one of his People having any Correspondence
at *Constantinople*, he desired to depart, and to pass
through the Emperor's Dominions ; which was
very readily granted him.

The Court of *Vienna* issued Orders, that the
whole Expence of him and his Retinue should be
every where defrayed , and they met with a very
honourable Reception in his Imperial Majesty's
Territories As to the King himself, having
followed the Emperor's Advice, rather to take a
long

long Journey round in the Empire, than to come near *Saxony*, he fet out with only one Officer, Lieutenant-Colonel *During*; and, without making himſelf any where known, he arrived on the fourteenth Day at *Stralſund*.

At his Arrival in that City, General *Ranck's* Negociation, for the Marriage of the hereditary Prince of *Heſſe-Caſſel*, which had been fet on Foot in *Turkey*, was brought to a Concluſion. The Landgrave himſelf came ſome time after to wait on the King, and made him ſome Propoſitions of Peace with King *Auguſtus* But, their Differences not being eaſy to reconcile, the Landgrave's Negociation had no Effect.

All the preceding Illuſtrations, as well upon the Loſs of the Battle of *Pultawa*, as upon many Events that happened in *Turkey*, will perhaps ſuffice to give new Light to the Author of the Hiſtory, concerning one of the greateſt Heroes of the Age, and the moſt extraordinary Man of our Times.

If he had out-lived the unfortunate Campaign in *Norway*, his Plan, for Deſigns much more ſurpriſing than any of the preceding, was entirely laid down, and ready for Execution, and his Peace with the Czar was already quite adjuſted, and ſo far advanced, that it wanted nothing but the Ratification.

F I N I S.

Ingram Content Group UK Ltd.
Milton Keynes UK
UKHW051206120323
418216UK00036B/135